To Cynthia,
May God be
your life as our
Love Always,
Denise

Opening
The Door

Second Printing

Denise Clayton Bryant

Opening
The Door

Denise Clayton Bryant

**The events and facts are true, but most names have been changed
to protect privacy of actual individuals.**

Second Printing 1998

PUBLISHED BY:
BRENTWOOD CHRISTIAN PRESS
4000 BEALLWOOD AVENUE
COLUMBUS, GEORGIA 31904

To God for His goodness, His grace, and His mercy, for without Him, I could not have passed the test; to my husband, Darrell, whose love has given me strength which even I didn't know I possessed; to my sons, Tjai, Christopher and Little Darrell, who make life worth living, in a challenging sort of way. I have come to realize that even after the greatest loss, life can, does and must continue. It's all a part of God's plan...and He is the Master Architect!

I also want to thank God for two of His very special angels... Patricia Gant and Luella Rhodes-Blount.

Introduction

My hearing was restored when I heard glass breaking in the kitchen and Grandmama's pantry shelves crashing to the floor! Grandmama and I peered around the doorway to see what was happening. The sight was a horrendous one! My father, Tony was a huge, dark, venomous creature, a monster covered in White Lily flour, from head to toe! In his hand was a revolver, black and threatening, as he crept slowly through the shotgun house! Mama was still there, holding the phone. They were in the same room! Once, Tony shot her in the leg and she fell down to the floor, still grasping the receiver! Her blood splattered on the wall! The black, wire phonestand fell over on the floor beside her.

Thirty-one years later, after my father shot and wounded my seven year old brother and our grandfather moments before brutally murdering my mother and grandmother and finally turning his .38 revolver on himself, I was united, for the first time, with a sister I never knew existed. My sister, Debra, held the key which unlocked the memories of that fateful night in November, 1966 and others that threatened to spiritually destroy me throughout the years. As I began to write, in search of healing and reconciliation with that past, Opening the Door, a testimony of faith and determination to overcome the Evil One, exploded from within me! With relentless honesty, the Holy Spirit has revealed God's call to witness upon my life. This is my testimony.

One

There is an inward spirit or consciousness that compels writers to write. Actor Billy Crystal said it over and over again, in the smash comedy, "Throw Momma from the Train," when he repeatedly quipped that "a writer writes... always." That, I suppose is true. I've been writing for a long time, although not always on paper, typewriter, or by way of computer. A lot of my writing has been on the tablets of my mind. Now, I find myself writing with sincere purpose. I am desperately in need of healing. I am writing in hopes of achieving that healing. True writers, I am sure, can relate.

I am convinced that every living soul needs healing of some sort. We have all been bruised and scarred at some point in our lives. We have all had experiences which we wish we had never had to undergo. We have all pushed some, if not all of those experiences into places deep within the recesses of our minds. I know that I am not the only person who has done this, but I must confess my guilt at having done so. I might add that storing these "skeletons" has not been without consequence. I suppose I am writing in an attempt to undo some of the damage and find some peace... some healing. At this point, I am not sure just how successful I will be. By the time I am finished, I should know.

Just when I thought I was beginning to make some rational sense of this abnormal life of mine, God threw me another curve! I recently described to someone my perception of the current tuft of events in my life as that of someone on the outside of an upstairs window, looking in. I am being supported by an unseen force as I peer through the sheer fabric of the curtains. The feeling is eerie, yet I am not afraid of the "force" because it is very familiar to me. I believe it has undergirded me for as long as I can remember.

My perspective is one which has manifested itself in my life numerous times in the past. I can clearly remember, one cold winter night in Ft. Dodge, Iowa, when I found myself, standing out on the front porch of our house, looking in through the window. I was about six or seven years old. It was very cold outside and there was snow on the ground. My father, Tony, on one of numerous angry rampages, had ordered me outside onto the front porch, clad only in my pajamas. I shivered, watching him through the worn sheers, once again, physically abusing my mother. For some obscure reason, he had not wanted me to see him hit her... this time. I don't know why this should have been any different from the many, many other times he had hit her in front me and my three brothers. On this particular night, I watched in fear, as he paced back and forth in front of her, like an enraged panther, ready to pounce upon his prey. The only reason he had not already hit her was that she was still holding my baby brother, Ronnie, in her arms. I can still hear Ronnie wailing, as he clung to our mother, Almarine.

When Tony realized that Mama was not going to put Ronnie down, he threw down the ashtray he had been holding and planning to hit her with, and stormed out of the house. He seemed not to notice me, standing there, shivering in the cold. As he thundered down the steps, Mama quickly rushed outside and ushered me into the house, out of the cold and into the warmth of her arms. Ronnie was still in one arm. He had stopped crying. I was just getting started. After that night, it seemed, I was always crying.

Oddly enough, during the most emotional times of my adult life, I have often found it very difficult to cry. Perhaps, my wells are dry because I have cried so many tears in the past. Emotional hurt does not normally draw tears from me, but anger, on the contrary, does. It is easier for me to cry when someone has really upset me than it is when my feelings are hurt. The only explanation I can come up with is that I have no tears left for hurt. That reservoir has long been expended. I wonder if that is normal.

*He that overcometh shall inherit all things; and I will be
his God, and he shall be my son. Rev. 21:7*

In February of 1997, I was forced to temporarily stop doing something I love --teaching. The incident, or should I say "incidents" which drove me away from my classroom and my students are very painful to me. One would think I would be accustomed to pain by now, after all of the experiences, mostly painful ones, that I have undergone in my lifetime. I suppose no one ever becomes immune to pain though. Each painful experience just seems to become a part of who we are and, for the most part, we learn to deal with it. I have discovered that the true test of character is when and how we deal with those experiences. Another test has been placed on the desk before me. I hope I can pass it!

I can remember my very first day in my own classroom. School began in August, 1995. As I stood in front of my new students, I wasn't nervous like I had expected to be. I was exhilarated! I kept thinking, "This is my classroom! These are my students!" I was overwhelmed and I think I probably overwhelmed my students, too. They kept giving me this "What is she so excited about?" look. I peered beyond their quizzical expressions and saw minds that were slightly ajar. I couldn't wait to start shoveling in that knowledge as my college professors had so aptly prepared me to do! I might need to interject here that although college professors equip new teachers to handle the content in their field of expertise, they don't actually prepare us rookies for the "real world" out there! But then, I guess they really can't. Who can predict what monstrosities each new generation of children will devise? The Scriptures have already warned us that every generation will be weaker and wiser. That means we have to be ready for just about anything!

My first year went spectacularly! I went from "day one" to "day one-hundred and eighty" full of vitality and exuberance! By the end of the year, most of my students had learned what I had so earnestly tried to teach them. Of course, there were some who had made up their minds on that same "day one" that they were not remotely interested in anything I had to say about " Bill

Shakespeare" or "Bob Dylan" or "Dylan Thomas" or whatever what's-his-face's name was. But there were some who told later me that they had had dreams of Julius Caesar and nightmares of that horrendous "Prologue to the Canterbury Tales!" I assured them that the nightmares would pass and if nothing else, they would always remember that funny things do happen on the way to the Forum!"

My oldest brother, Wayne, reminded me, sometime during my first year teaching, that he had always known I would end up being a teacher. He said that because I had spent many days on the front porch of our little house on Twenty-Second Street, playing school and insisting that he and our two younger brothers, Michael and Ronnie, play students. Secondly, Wayne said that, in his opinion, I always did think I knew everything and he was sure that was just too much knowledge for any one person to keep to themselves! I, on the other hand, can't remember ever having really wanted to become a teacher until a few years ago.

"Trust in the Lord with all thine heart; and lean not unto thine own understanding." Prov. 3:5

While residing in Los Angeles, one Sunday morning in the Spring of 1990, I stood in the doorway of the Carthage United Methodist Church's Youth Sunday School classroom and challenged some teenage kids in the class once more before leaving the room. We had been discussing the Scripture which admonishes us to "Choose ye this day whom ye will serve." I wanted to help them to see that those ageless words were very relevant in the 90's and could not let the opportunity to do so slip by. "So just what do you think the "Bloods" and "Crips" mean when they ask what 'set' you're with?" I asked the teenagers.

The Bloods and Crips were local Los Angeles gangs with whom we had all been made much too familiar because of their constant warring with each other in the communities around us and the innocent lives that had been lost as a result. The kids knew all about that. They knew about the brandishing of colors by respective gang members in the neighborhoods which they had claimed as their "turf." I knew that some of the kids in that Sunday School class had even been asked to join gangs themselves. One of the boys asked me what my comment had to do with the Sunday School lesson. We had been talking about the choices kids had to make. I stepped back inside the classroom door and looked squarely at him.

"If you say 'yes' to Satan, aren't you saying 'no' to God?" I asked.

He nodded.

"If you say 'yes' to the Bloods or the Crips, isn't that just like saying 'no' to God, too?"

"How's that?" he asked. He looked interested enough for me to continue.

I got a little "rush" just knowing that somebody wanted to know something from me. "Gang members sell drugs to people, even children. They have killed many innocent people. They've also robbed and destroyed people's homes, too. Haven't they?" I asked.

He nodded his head again, in agreement.

"Well," I went on, "who else does the Bible describe as seeking to destroy, rob and murder innocent people?" I looked around at the ardent faces in the room.

The kids were silent.

"Think about it," I said with a smile. Not really expecting an answer, I turned to leave the room. "I'll see you guys next Sunday." With that, I left them alone, realizing that I had caused something in their hearts and minds to stir. They would think about what I had said. That much, I knew. I hoped they would remember its significance. And maybe, at a much needed time, they would be able to make a choice - the right choice! I realized that something else had happened in that room, too. Something happened to me! As I walked away from the still, silent classroom, I felt that I was on the verge of discovering what I really wanted to do with my life!

"In all thy ways acknowledge him, and he shall direct thy path." Prov. 3:6

When I graduated from high school in 1976, like most of my friends, I went away to college. My GPA and SAT scores were high enough, so I was accepted into Mercer University in Macon, Georgia. Enthusiastically, I started school in the fall. I went to Mercer for all of one semester, until I was suddenly overcome by what I interpreted as mass chaos in my life! I felt out of place and very much out of sync. I remember my roommate's reaction when I announced, after some thought, that I was going home. Trina was devastated, as were many other friends I had made at school, that I was just "dropping out!" I couldn't explain to anyone why I felt it was necessary for me to go home. I really didn't know the reason why. I just felt so compelled to do so that my luggage was packed and stacked in our tiny dormitory room for nearly two weeks before the Dean finally agreed to allow me to withdraw in good standing.

I had gone to the prestigious Georgia university to begin studies which would prepare me for a career in Political Science some day. I had flatly refused to consider a future in music because it seemed that the only career I could pursue with certainty would be in Music Education. Me, be a teacher? No way, I thought! I had been writing songs and playing the piano since the age of eight. Everyone, and I do mean everyone, assumed that I would make music my career. In high school, I had turned down a music scholarship because I did not want to go that route, simply because everyone expected me to. My mom used to say that I always did the opposite of what I was told. I guess she had a point. She also said that I always seemed to be where I was not supposed to be. In retrospect, I guess that has been the case, more often than not. In any event, I had no intention of tapping out the years of my life with a baton, keeping time for some enthusiastic mother's "wannabe prodigy!"

I returned to Columbus and got a job. In the Spring of 1977, I enrolled at nearby Columbus College, once again, declaring myself a Political Science major. All of my classes were in the evening. I tried, but I could not stay away from the Fine Arts Hall, leaving my two-hour class at the break each night, and most times, not returning to class that evening. Every night, I closed myself up in one of the practice rooms, away from the world. I played the piano for hours, writing songs and somehow searching to fill the void in my soul. I soon found myself dissatisfied with school, with life, and with myself! At that time, I thought my dissatisfaction was caused by something or someone out to get me! Nevertheless, I kept at it until October, 1978, when I eventually dropped out of college for the second time! I moved to Atlanta, Georgia to find myself. There, in the busy city, I found everything, but me!

Early in 1979, I became a lead vocalist and keyboard player with an Atlanta-based Rhythm & Blues band. At the same time, I was holding down a job as Director of Music at a Methodist church, as well. These seemingly "conflicting" occupations were quite a challenge for me - especially on weekends when the band performed out of town. Even while we were on the road, we would always have to speed back to Atlanta before day some Sunday mornings to "get me to the church on time!" The other members of the band, all males, never complained though. They were a great bunch of guys! Most of the time, they treated me like a little sister. They said they understood how it was with a "good Christian girl" because that's what they thought I was. So, they never offered me any of their marijuana or cocaine. They never let anyone else offer it to me either!

On various occasions, I sat in the dressing room and watched them and other entertainers "get high" between "sets" on Friday and Saturday nights. Once we backed up a well-known entertainer at an Atlanta night club. Before the show, she generously offered me and the other female singer in the group some cocaine that had been liberally spread out on the dressing room table. The other young lady immediately "snorted" a line of fine, white powder. I declined to indulge. I had never been into drugs and saw no reason to get started on what I was sure was a downward path! When I refused the cocaine, she produced two "reefers" and asked me if I smoked "weed."

"No," I replied.

11

"Well," the very attractive woman asked, a sly smile crossing her ruby red lips, "What do you do?"

"I sing," I said, returning her smile.

I found it quite amazing that after she had gotten high, she came out before the audience and literally sang her butt off! I was so awed that I could scarcely remember the words that Annie and I were supposed to be singing as we backed her up! I stumbled badly during the hour performance, but oddly enough, no one on the stage seemed to notice!

On each Sunday morning that followed our weekend performances, I would sit on a bench at the piano and play the songs of Zion through partially-closed eyelids. Some people actually thought I was "in the Spirit" when my eyes were closed. My friend, Casey, who was a member of the choir, knew that it was just exhaustion from the previous night's gig.

A lot of things changed for me in the years from 1978 to 1985. I "left" a lot things. I had already left school. I had recently left home, and I eventually left the band. We were no longer hearing the same beat. The other members seemed to be more interested in the female following than the future of the group. Their goals and mine did not appear to be the same - not that I really knew what my goals were. But I was convinced that I wanted and needed more out of the business. So, I made a decision to venture out on my own. I quit. For what seemed like a "few minutes," I went solo and did a few stints at a local piano bar. It seemed pretty cool at the time and I was momentarily content. After all, I was still making music.

In 1982, I made what was probably the worse mistake of my entire life. I married someone who was very much like my father. My father was not a bad man - he was horrible! Since beginning this self-therapy, I have discovered that he was even worse than I had imagined. After all of the destruction and havoc he wreaked upon my life and my other family members, you would think I would be able to spot his likeness at least a dozen miles off. But no... I was still looking for myself and instead, I found a husband. The union was disastrous and after a year and a half and a son, I was finally able to get out of the bed of thorns I had made for myself. It was by no means an easy task, but I managed to get away safely, my eighth month old son in tow.

In January, 1985, I left my father's clone and returned home to Columbus. When I arrived, I had no intentions of staying there permanently. I just needed to get somewhere and sit down just long enough to get myself together. They say you can always go back home. Perhaps you can, but it is never the same and neither are you. Unfortunately, your parents are not aware of that. They expect you to slide back into adolescent mode and keep your curfew. And you, the adult you have become, expect them to leave you alone and let you do whatever it is you think you want to do. I came home and found that I could not stay very long. I realized that I no longer felt "at home" and the realization was quite devastating to me! If "home" was no longer "home," then where in the world was "home?"

Filled with a new desperation to find my place in the word, I packed my then thirteen-month old son and all of our worldly possessions in a U-Haul trailer hitched to the back of my Chevrolet Cavalier and struck out west to California! The trip was long and tedious. I found myself unable to do very much driving after the sun went down each of the four days we spent on the road. My youngest brother, Ronnie, accompanied Tjai and me on the trip. I taught him how to drive my four-speed Cavalier on the long stretch of highway between Birmingham, Alabama and Fort Worth, Texas. On the fourth of July, we pulled over to the side of the interstate and watched, along with other travelers, the breathtaking display of fireworks in the midnight blue sky over El Paso, Texas. After much driving and stopping and driving and stopping, we finally arrived in Los Angeles on July 5th, around midnight.

In the City of Angels, I spent many long hours and countless days, sitting on the beach, staring out at the waves, wondering what to do next. I discovered that the ocean is a beautiful creation. God had to have made it. Man is incapable of such perfection! Even the waters of the Pacific, dirty and polluted by

13

mankind, appear to be pretty, tantalizing shades of blue, the farther out you look. Some days, I sat and meditated, hoping that God would show some mercy and send me a message in a bottle, washed up on the shores of Manhattan Beach. I kept one eye on my son, Tjai, frolicking at the water's edge and the other on the white, foamy tide, looking for a message... looking for the bottle. It never appeared. After a while, I would collect my things, shaking the gritty white sand from my feet and legs and carry my squirming, protesting toddler to the car. Tjai loved the beach - the sand and the sea! After a while, I gave up and stopped looking for the bottle and just enjoyed watching him play in the water.

"Be ye therefore followers of God, as dear children."
Eph. 5:1

The other day, I told my husband, Darrell, that everyone has a talent. He had been complaining that he had not discovered what his talent actually was. We both agreed that, in time, everyone's talent would be manifested, in some way or another. Some talents are easily seen, taken advantage of and appreciated. Others take a little time to surface. I assured Darrell that God had not left him out. He is a very talented artist. He insisted that his ability was learned. I disagreed with him on that. I believe that had there not been something there in the first place, there would have been nothing to develop! It's all about time - that's the rhythm of life!

During my residency in Los Angeles, I wrote several articles which appeared in the "Mohammed Speaks" Newspaper. I have always loved to write! My articles dealt with subject material with which I was well acquainted. Primarily, I wrote about the experience of being a Black woman in America and the pride and dignity of the race. I had been attending weekly lectures at a mosque in East Los Angeles at the invitation of a Muslim friend of mine. I found the lectures about the experience of Blacks in America very interesting and quite enlightening. The minister diligently sought to add me to the number of his congregation at the mosque. He thought that I would be a tremendous asset to the Nation of Islam.

14

Although I felt intellectually stimulated for having attended lectures there, I could not whole-heartedly accept the teachings of the "Honorable Elijah Mohammed" and therefore, I could not trade my life of Christianity for a life of Islam. I told the members of the mosque, many with whom I had become very good friends, that I could not easily discard what I had been taught all of my life. In the depths of my soul, I knew that God was the God of the Scriptures! I could not accept their version and I was one-hundred percent sure that I was not about to convert them to Christianity. So I continued to attend the Sunday afternoon lectures and I continued to listen - intellectually. When I was asked whether or not I was willing to accept their doctrine, I declined. As I knew they would, they accepted my decision with the dignity that had initially earned them my respect, but still encouraged me to write for their newspaper. The "Mohammed Speaks" Newspaper headquarters was located in Atlanta.

When I left Los Angeles in November of 1990, I intended to return to Atlanta to live. It was not in God's plan, however, for me to stay there. A week after my arrival there, Aunt Meg, my "mom" who had raised my brothers and I after our biological parents died, suffered a heart attack, so I moved to Columbus. God was moving, strategically putting things into their proper place. He was setting the stage, pouring the foundation for what He knew was yet to come. I didn't know it, but His plan had long been set into motion.

I ended up living in Columbus, caring for my dad, Harry, after Aunt Meg's death. I resigned myself to the fact that I would not be going back to Atlanta. With calm resolve, I decided to stay put and let God have His way. In my nightly prayers, I began to ask Him what He wanted me to do. I was willing, I confessed, to do it, whatever it might be, if He would only lay upon my heart what "it" actually was!

I had been in Columbus for about two months when I decided the time had come for me to go back to college. I enrolled at Columbus College, but I was undecided about what course of study I would undertake. When asked to declare a major, I simply checked the box marked "Undecided," because that's exactly what I was! At registration, I saw a former professor who chided me with "Better late than never, Clayton!" I laughed, but I felt strange that day. For the first time in my life, I actually felt like I was where I was supposed to be.

The first day of class, I walked over to the Registrar's office to change the "Undecided" on my transcript to "Secondary Education-English." When I told my dad that, he was surprised. He thought I would go into music, based upon my heavy background in music. I had been playing the piano and singing since the age of eight. I told him that I wanted to teach English because I believed that the students who took music were usually pretty good students, creative and ambitious. I wanted to touch the lives of the ones who might otherwise "fall between the cracks." What better way to do that than to teach a subject that everyone was required to take? English!

In California, I had seen young people, some high school graduates, who had difficulty reading, were unable to accurately complete job applications or write their own resumes - abilities which are essential for survival in these times! With a passion unlike any I had ever experienced in my life, I threw myself completely into school! For the first time, I honestly felt the rhythm of my life coming into an even meter of its own.

By the time I met Darrell, I was well on my way towards finding my beat. I think he sensed that in me. He once told me that what attracted him to me was that I seemed to know what I wanted. I almost laughed! It seemed to me that just the day before, I was sitting on the beach, anxiously staring out at the waves. When we were married in November of 1992, I knew that he was part of the plan. Looking into his eyes on our wedding day gave me a warm, comfortable feeling - like the one babies get from sucking their thumbs, maybe.

Once, I heard someone say that you don't choose your career but rather, your career chooses you. I would take that a step further. While you are yet a thumb-sucking fetus in your mother's womb, your career path has already been set for you. The confusion sets in when you get off the beat, determined to go what you think is your own way. That's what gang members have done. They have gotten off the beat. Drug dealers, too! They stepped off the beat and now they think they own the whole blasted song! I had asked the kids in that Sunday School class about gang membership because I knew they were familiar with that. I wanted to make the Word of God relative to their own lives. In doing so, I saw myself, off of the beat that had already been established for me. For years, I danced, sang and played around it - doing things I wasn't supposed to do and finding myself in places where I wasn't supposed to be. I was looking for a message in a bottle, waiting to discover my purpose. Somehow, I think I would have found myself sooner, had I followed my young son's example and dared to jump in and at least, get my feet wet, amidst the syncopated rhythms of life!

In the Fall of 1996, having had a pretty successful first year, I decided to return to the same school for a second year. I felt that my efforts had benefited the students and saw no reason to fix something that didn't need fixing. So, despite offers from the system closest to home, I resumed my thirty-something-miles-each-way-every-day commute to school for another term.

With very few exceptions, I had almost all new students! I had two Freshman English classes, three Sophomore English Classes and one Senior English class. Some of the tenth grade students had taken Freshman English from me the previous year and they were well acquainted with my teaching methods. They warned their fellow classmates that they had better "get with the program" because they would have to earn any grades they expected to get in my class. A lot of the students, who had never been in my class before, complained that my expectations were "too high." They argued that they had not been expected to do so much work in their other classes and saw no reason why I should expect them to do it for me! I struggled to get my students to expect more from themselves than they were accustomed to. I encouraged them to challenge themselves to achieve more than they had planned to when they entered class

17

on the first day. I told them about myself and my struggle to become a teacher. Some of them wanted to know why I opted to teach there, in their small rural town, instead of going to teach at one of the schools in Columbus, where I lived. I told them that I was there because of them. That was all there was to it.

It was a challenge just getting them motivated. They were not as interested in learning as the students I had taught the previous year. By the time Christmas holidays rolled around, things began to shape up, though. My kids realized that I was serious about teaching, so they would do well to get serious about learning... particularly my Freshmen. The Sophomores painstakingly whined their way through the Research Paper unit during the fourth six weeks grading period. Nearly every student turned in their final paper on time. I was elated! The students who failed to turn their papers in were the ones whom I had already known had no intentions of turning one in when we had first begun. I had watched them idly waste their time and "goof off" in the Media Center when they should have been doing active research. After a couple of warnings, I left them alone. I had already led the horses to water...

In my Freshman class, I had several students who were older than they should have been in the ninth grade. Among those students were some who had been moved up from the sixth or seventh grades the previous year to the ninth grade. I wasn't quite sure what to do with them. Obviously, if they had not been able to do sixth, seventh, or eighth grade work, they would have a difficult time trying to do ninth grade work! I tried to monitor their work a little more closely than the other students, without calling too much attention to them.

One of my students, whom I will call "David," was not in class very often. When he did come to school, he would usually get suspended before the end of the day. He was an older student, about seventeen, who was in my sixth period ninth grade English class. David was not really disruptive during class, other than talking a little too much when the class was involved in cooperative or group learning activities. Often he openly admitted that although we should be honored by the presence of his company, he simply was not going to do any work in class or otherwise! He usually sat and contributed a wise crack or two during the class period. The other students usually laughed or snickered at his comments. They all seemed to like him well enough. Of course, the town was very small and everyone knew everyone else anyway.

One Tuesday in February, 1997, David showed up at school. The bell rang for the sixth period class to begin and at the very start of class, I had a problem with a female student. She was being very disrespectful towards me. I was shocked because I had never had any problem with her before. "Lisa" was usually a very sweet, cooperative student. On that particular day, she became very angry and quite belligerent with me because I would not excuse her to go to another teacher's room to work on an assignment during my class period. I expressed to her that my class was equally as important as any other class she had, so I expected her to be in class when she was scheduled to be. Her attitude became very ugly and her disposition extremely rude. I took Lisa outside of the classroom to talk to her privately. I didn't want to chastise her in front of her classmates. Once we were outside of the room, I closed the door and spoke quietly, but firmly, to her.

I tried to reason with Lisa, but she simply glared at me and snatched her head away, as if she could have cared less what I had to say. After a few moments, I gave up and sent her on to the office. I returned to the classroom and asked the other students to remain quiet until I came back. Then I left to accompany Lisa to the assistant principal's office.

After the assistant principal, Mr. Edwards, talked with the young lady, she apologized to me in his presence, and I accepted her apology. I really believed that she was sincere. When she began to cry, I fought hard to resist the temptation to reach out and comfort her. As I left her in the office to return to my class, I felt badly for having taken her to the office. She had never given me any trouble before.

19

When I returned to my classroom, I immediately got started. I asked the students to take out their vocabulary words so that we could review for an upcoming test. All of the students complied, except David. He was turned around in his seat, arguing with another student. I could hear the other student, "Randy," speaking back to David. Randy's soft voice was calm as he responded to David's chiding him. I asked David to turn around in his seat and be quiet so that we could go on with the class. Reluctantly, he got up and strolled, casually, around the aisle of desks to the one he had been sitting backwards in. Randy was now silent, taking out his vocabulary words. David sat down, but continued speaking to Randy.

"David," I said, sternly, "please be quiet and leave him alone."

"He's about to get slapped in here!" he snapped, to no one in particular.

"Not in here," I said, looking directly at him.

"Uh huh," he retorted, "so he'd better shut up!" His voice was thick and a little slower than usual.

I stood behind my podium in front of the class and told David that no one was going to get slapped in my classroom.

"Well," he continued, "I'll take him outside then. Either way, he's going to get slapped!" He was looking at me now.

"No," I said, "You're not going to take him outside either."

Then he said something that caught me totally off guard. "You just need to stop talking to me, B----!"

The words slapped me hard in the face! The entire class gasped! For a moment, I could not respond. When I was able to speak, I said, as calmly as I could, "You need to get up and leave the room."

"You not making me go nowhere, B----!" He spat the words at me.

I could not believe that he was talking to me! Again, I told him to leave the room.

He didn't budge.

When I realized that he was not going to move, I walked over to the door and began pressing the call button to summon help from the main office. I pressed the button four, five, six times... No one responded in the office. I pressed it a few more times... Still no response! I knew that all of the students, including David, were watching me and saw my futile efforts. No one was coming to my assistance. I could feel perspiration building in the pits of my underarms.

David got up from his seat and started towards me. "You're just a b----!" He walked closer and closer to me. He was so close, I could see his nostrils flaring. "I'm not scared of you," he said, standing directly in front of me. His nose was touching mine now.

I could smell the mustiness of his clothes and feel his breath, hot on my face. "I'm not scared of you, either," I managed to say. My heart was racing! Keeping my eyes on him, I continued to press the call button a few more times. Still, there was no answer. I could not imagine where the staff was or what they could possibly be doing, not to have heard the buzzer that I was sure was screaming in the office!

David thrust his hands deep into the pockets of his baggy pants. My eyes darted frantically from his pockets to the menacing expression on his face as he continued to curse foully in my face.

"I bet you're gonna tell them that I hit you, ain't you?"

He was asking me a question? How ludicrous, I thought. I didn't answer. In fact, I said nothing else to him. I didn't want him to have any reason to retaliate against me. My lips were sealed and my eyes fixed on him.

"That's okay," he said, "'Tell them I hit you! I'm gonna come back and bash your head in!"

I was near panic! I grabbed the doorknob and turned it, opening the door just a crack. I tried to see out into the hall, hoping that someone, anyone, might be able to come to my aid. Where was everyone? Usually, there was always somebody in the hall. Now, when I desperately needed someone to be there, there was not a soul in sight! Quickly, I spun around to face David. I couldn't afford to take my eyes off of him for long, in case he had something in his pockets, a knife, a gun, anything that could hurt me or even possibly take my life! I thought about my children. What would happen to them if something happened to me? Who would rear them? Help them? Love them? For a split second, I thought about my own childhood. I had needed my own mother so many times and she had not been there. Life was rock hard and ice cold with no "mama" to comfort or console me. I didn't want that for my children!

As I turned back to David, he grabbed me! I didn't know if he planned to throw me down on the floor or out into the hall! I could hear my other students in the room, shouting for him to stop and to leave me alone. I don't think he heard them and I'm pretty sure, he cared even less! Before I knew what was happening, he had thrust me hard against the doorway! I stumbled backwards, into the hall. We were out there, David and me, alone! The door closed behind us, between him and me and my students! My heart was racing!

"I'm gonna get you!" he snarled at me as he headed briskly to the nearest exit from the building.

I backed away from him and headed, as fast as my legs could carry me, to the nearest phone, in the Media Center. By the time I got there, my emotions had skyrocketed! I asked the Media Specialist if I could use the phone in her office. She stared at me as if I had three heads or something! I could hear her asking me what was wrong, but I couldn't answer. I needed what was left of my calm to call the principal. She led me to the phone in her office. I sat down at her desk, picked up the receiver and dialed.

After two rings, the principal answered. I could feel myself becoming light-headed. I was beginning to hyperventilate. I spoke into the mouthpiece and found it hard to breathe. I gasped for air as I tried to explain to the principal what had just occurred. Frantically, I asked him to call the police.

The principal seemed to recognize my voice on the phone rather slowly. "Mrs. Bryant?" he said, somewhat cautiously.

I told him that I had been attacked by a student and that I needed him to call the police right away.

"What's wrong, Mrs. Bryant?" he asked, in his usual calm manner.

I repeated that I had been attacked by a student. I asked him to call the police. He asked me where I was and I told him. Then I slammed down the phone and plunged, headlong, into hysteria! I don't remember very clearly what happened next. Vaguely, I recall a fellow teacher, standing over me, saying "Breathe, Dee!" over and over again. I had lost any trace of my composure by that time. I was still having a hard time catching my breath.

An hour later, at a local doctor's office, my blood pressure was still one sixty over one hundred. A kind-faced nurse came into the examination room and took pictures of my arms with a Polaroid camera. Large bruises had begun to form on my inner arm regions. She told me that the pictures would be placed in my file. She apologized for what had happened to me before leaving the room.

The doctor came in and talked to me. In his calm, reserved manner, he told me that he would prescribe something to help me to calm down. I knew that the only thing that would really calm me down was for me to get away from there - away from the school, the community, the town! I needed to get away from there as quickly as possible!

The superintendent and an employee from the board office drove me the thirty-eight miles home. I had expressed a desire to call Darrell, but the superintendent suggested that I wait until I got home. He felt that by the time I reached home, I would have calmed down and perhaps, Darrell would not get as angry as he probably would have if I had talked to him in my current state. I understood his reasoning, but I really wanted to talk to my husband! All the way home, I kept visualizing David, standing in front of me, threatening me and calling me 'b----!' By the time I got there, I was still a wreck!

Darrell wasn't home. The superintendent told me to ask Darrell to call him at home when he got there. I told him that I would. I went inside the house and went straight to the telephone to call my brother-in-law's house, where I knew my husband would most likely be. I asked my sister-in-law if he was there. He was.

"I need to talk to him," I said, trying to speak calmly.

"What's wrong?" my sister-in-law, April, asked, sensing something amiss in my tone of voice.

"I was attacked by a student today," I replied.

"What?!"

"I need to talk to Darrell," I said, my voice breaking.

Immediately, she summoned him to the phone.

Before I could get the words out of my mouth, Darrell said, "I'll be there in a minute." He slammed down the phone.

I did not return to school for a little over a week. By then, the ugly bruises on my arms and back were almost invisible. When I went back, I tried to behave as normally as I could, but it was very difficult. David's threat was never very far away from my mind. I tried to get back into the swing of things with my other students. I didn't want them to suffer because of one student's actions. They knew I was trying. I could sense that they were trying, too.

On Friday of my first week back, another incident occurred. This time, a student, who was very angry about having been excluded from a field trip to a play, approached me in a very rude and hostile manner. I had been one of the Literary Club advisors and the group was scheduled to go to Columbus to see a play that day. As the students boarded the big yellow school bus that morning, another one of my freshman students walked up to me and asked why I had left him off of the list. The young man had just been released from In-School Suspension that morning. I told him hat I had not known he wanted to go. Besides that, he had been in "PASS" during the time when the other students were signing up for the trip. By the time he got out, the list was complete and the bus was filled to maximum capacity. There were simply no vacant seats on the bus. I tried to explain that to him as quickly as I could, as students filed onto the bus behind us. He became very belligerent and demanded that either he be allowed to get on the bus or that I give him back the five dollars he had paid to attend an earlier play. We had not been able to go to that one because it had been canceled. I told the student that I could not let him get on the bus, nor did I have his money. I said, however, that I would see about getting him his money back on the following Monday. Hurriedly, I explained that after the money had been collected, three months earlier, it had been turned into the district office. Clubs were not allowed to keep money at the school. He glared at me and screamed that he didn't care what I said, I was going to give him his money back or else!

"Or else what?" I asked, frowning.

"You'd better give me my d----- money!" he yelled into my face.

Some of the students who were waiting to board the bus, and some who had been standing around the rising commotion between him and I, turned their attention to us. For a few seconds, I stared back at him, unable to believe that I was so soon again under attack.

He fell silent. I turned and walked away from him, in the direction of the main office. Inside, I asked the secretary for a discipline referral form. She didn't have any, but suggested I write the incident down on a sheet of paper and told me that would suffice. She handed me a clean sheet of lineless paper and I walked into the teacher's mailbox room. I sat down at the long wooden table there, and recorded what had just occurred. After I had scrawled the student's name and brief details of the incident on the paper, I left the main building to take it to the assistant principal's office. He was busy with another student, so I couldn't get in to see him at the moment. I knew that the bus should be loaded and ready to go, so I handed the paper to his secretary and asked her to see that he got it. When I went back outside to get on the bus, the student had disappeared.

The school day was over by the time we returned from seeing the play. The last bell had already sounded and most of the students had left the building. I went to my classroom to pick up my things and prepare for the long drive home. As I entered the section of the building where my room was, I noticed that a few students were still lingering in the hallway near my door. The student with whom I had had the confrontation earlier that day was one of them. Because of his behavior that morning, he had been suspended, but he was still at school. Unsurprisingly, his bitterness had escalated. As I approached my door, he resumed his earlier argument, saying that it was my fault that he had not been able to go on the trip. He was still bent on getting his money back. He threatened to do whatever he needed to do in order to get it back... from me.

I reminded the student that I had already discussed the issue with him earlier that day and that I had no intention of discussing it any further. He became so loud and so hostile that a couple of the students who had been witnessing this confrontation grabbed hold of him and pulled him towards the exit, away from me. It was a very familiar scenario. I could feel a thick cloud of tension in the air. The irate student was being dragged from the same door that David had gone through, just after he had assaulted me, less than two weeks ago! I felt a very uncomfortable presence, standing there in the hall. Suddenly, I lost all rational thought. I became enraged! I was ready to fight back! In my mind, I told myself that I no longer cared about the job! I was not going to let another "child" hit me! Hell, I thought, I had children of my own at home that I spanked. I was not about to let a kid spank me! If he wanted to fight me, I was ready to fight back!

"Let him go!" I said, in a voice that was not my own.

All three of the students froze in their tracks!

"Let him go!" I repeated. "If he wants me, I'm standing right here!" This time, I sneered at him. "Just come over here and get me!" I challenged him. "Come on! Do it! Do it so that I can stomp your a-- into the ground!" I was shouting.

The students stared at me, unable to believe the transformation that was taking place before their very eyes! Obvious astonishment showed on their faces. The one who threatened me had now been threatened by me! He didn't know how to take it.

"Come on!" I urged him again. "I'm right here!"

For a moment, his eyes met mine. Then, I guess he realized that I was dead serious. He allowed the other two students take him through the doorway.

I stood there, looking after them. I was really angry! I knew that if that boy had come near me, I would have lost my job! I would have defended myself, at all costs! I had made up my mind that if he hit me, he was going to have a well-whipped behind that day! I had reached my limit! I had had enough!

I went to the Media Center to call Darrell. I told him about the second encounter. He told me to come home right away, but I knew that I was too upset to drive home right then. It was raining like mad outside, so I told him that I would be on shortly.

I went back to my room. I unlocked the door and went inside. Leaning against the door, I looked around at my students' projects, which were on display in the room. My eyes swept over the signs and bulletin board displays I had put up to motivate my students to achieve and excel. I thought about my commitment to teaching those kids and the brick wall that I had run up against while trying to do so. I felt very much alone in that room. I felt very much alone in that school! I knew that God had to have known what was going on my life. He must! Something deep within moved me to take down some of my room decor. I went to the chalkboard and began removing the letters I had strategically placed over it. The letters said "Free Knowledge... Bring Your Own Container." I had put them there, over the chalkboard, knowing that each and every day, my students would sit in their desks and face those words. Perhaps, I thought, they would work like those fast food commercials which subliminally condition us to believe that we can have it our way and no matter what, we simply can't eat just one! I felt a tremendous sense of failure. Obviously, I had not been able to reach everyone. As I removed the letters, I found myself speaking aloud.

"I know this is not what you want for me, Lord!" I said. "Please do something! I cannot go on like this!" Tears ran down my cheeks. I realized that, once again, I was somewhere I didn't belong. I asked God for a solution to the problem, which had now become too big for me to handle.

Over the weekend, I complained to Darrell that since my return to school, several of the young men in my senior class had begun to drift into class late, following our lunch period. They had begun to come in ten to fifteen minutes after the rest of the class had returned from lunch. They would stroll through the doorway, go to their respective seats and sit down, as if their delayed entrance was a matter of habit! I wondered what they thought they were doing!

I returned to school on Monday, waiting to hear from God. Before the day was over, I did! Another student, this time, a senior, had gone berserk in my room. Darrell had come to the school to talk to my students. This was nothing unusual because he had done so on numerous occasions. This time, he brought his brother, Jerry, with him. They came to my classroom after lunch.

Darrell greeted the students and told them that he wanted to talk with them for a few moments. They were very attentive as he spoke. They were all well-acquainted with him. Darrell expressed his concern for my safety in the school, as well as the obvious disrespect being shown me by some of my seniors. Four of them walked into the room while he was talking with the class. Darrell saw the boys come into the room, but did not acknowledge them. He kept talking, encouraging the students to take advantage of the level of teaching I was attempting to give them. He told them that, in me, they had a teacher who genuinely cared about them and told them they should appreciate that. As he spoke, Darrell noticed that one of the students who had come in late and was now seated in the back of the classroom had begun "tossing gang signs" to no one in particular. He commented that "calling yourself a gang member" wasn't anything to be proud of either. The student became extremely hostile.

"What is he talking to me for?" he asked, looking around at his peers.

"I wasn't talking to anyone in particular," Darrell said. "I was just making a comment that being in a gang was nothing to be proud of." As he spoke, he gestured with his hands. Darrell, like many other people, uses his hands when he talks.

"You need to stop pointing at me," the young man retorted.

28

Jerry, who had been quiet up until that moment commented, "No one was pointing at you, son." He pivoted on the stool which he had been sitting on so that he could face the student. "But so what if someone points at you? If I pointed at you, it wouldn't hurt you, would it?" He demonstrated by pointing in the direction of the student. "See? That doesn't mean anything and it doesn't hurt you, does it?"

The student sprang up from his desk. "Somebody better tell that man to stop pointing at me!" He began to shove his books and other materials into his bookbag. He wasn't even supposed to have had that bookbag in class. It was against school policy for students to carry them. They were to be left in the students' lockers. The policy had been established in order to prevent students from carrying drugs or concealed weapons into the school. This student had a bookbag! I didn't think about it then, but now, I wonder just what he had in that bag!

By now, he had become incensed. "Somebody better tell that man to stop pointing at me before I bust a cap in his a--!" he yelled. He had finished stuffing his belongings into his bookbag and was now heading for the door. The other students appeared to be in shock at their peer's sudden display of anger.

I got up from my desk and called to him, but he ignored me and kept walking. I followed him out into the hallway and continued to call his name, asking him to stop so that I could talk to him. When I realized that he had no intention of stopping to talk to me, I turned and went in the other direction, towards the assistant principal's office. Once again, I needed his help! Once again, he was tied up with another discipline problem. I opened the door to the secretary's office and went inside.

She was sitting at her desk, pouring over a stack of papers.

"Does he have someone in there with him?" I asked the secretary.

She nodded, not even looking up from a stack of papers on her desk.

"Would you ask him to come and see me when he has a minute?"

She nodded again, still not looking up.

I left the office to return to my classroom. As I turned to go through the double doors which led out into the breezeway, I saw the "bookbag" on the arm of my irate student. He was standing beneath an awning, looking very flustered and talking to the Business Education teacher. I walked up to them. He was intently giving her his version of what had just transpired in my room. His version was not quite accurate.

I interrupted, "Why did you act like that?"

He turned to me. "That man was pointing at me!" he said.

"No," I retorted, "he wasn't. He was just trying to show you how silly it was for you to get upset about someone pointing at you. He was trying to show you that it couldn't possibly hurt you!"

He looked away angrily and mumbled something under his breath.

I waited for his next comment, but there was none.

Without another word, he turned and stormed off in the direction of the band room.

Exasperated, I looked at the other teacher. "I can't do this!" I cried, feeling defeated.

She looked at me apologetically. "I'm so sorry," she said.

"I have to go!" I cried. I turned and went into the building. I walked past my classroom and went to the Media Center. I picked up the phone and dialed the principal's office. When he answered, I asked him to please get someone to cover my classes. I told him that I was going to go home. I had taken about as much as I could. My tone of voice convinced him that I had reached the end of my rope. He must have known it. He told me that he would find someone to cover my classes. I hung up the phone and went back to my room.

My fifth period students had gone and my sixth period class had just come in. Upon entering the classroom, I told Darrell and Jerry that I was going home. The students asked me what had happened. Several of them wanted to know where I was going and why.

I just mumbled, "I have to go," and began collecting a few of my belongings to take with me. When it became evident to the students that I was leaving to go home, a lot of them began to cry! Some were screaming, begging me not to leave. My heart was breaking! As Darrell, Jerry and I left, five or six of the girls in my class followed us out into the hall and through the double-doors.

The same teacher was still standing outside, beneath the awning.

"Mrs. Bryant," she said, putting a hand on my arm to stop me, "These children need you." On her face was genuine concern.

I looked at her, tears welling up in my eyes. "I know," I said, my voice trembling, "but I can't go on like this! It's too much! My children at home need me, too." With that, I turned and hurried away from her and the children who were assembled just outside of the door.

"Mrs. Bryant!" someone called out to me, "Please don't leave!"

Another voice rang out, "Please Mrs. B., don't leave us! We need you!"

I knew that they needed me, but I needed something, too. I needed some peace of mind! I knew that I would never be able to find it there again. As we walked away, I could still hear the children's voices crying out to me, but I could not stay. They wanted me to be there for them, but I knew I would never be able to be there for them again.

"But as for you, ye thought evil against me, but God meant it unto good, to bring to pass, as it is this day, to save much people alive." Gen. 50:20

I had been away from school for about three weeks when I made an incredible discovery. I found out, at the age of thirty-eight, that I have a sister, who is also thirty-eight years old! We are not twins, somehow miraculously separated at birth. In fact, we are a mere two months apart! Prior to her phone call to tell me who she was, I had no inkling, in my wildest dreams, that I had ever had a sister! All my life, there was Wayne, Michael, Ronnie and me. My three brothers also believed that I was their only sister!

"You need to come to the phone and talk to this woman," Darrell said, standing in the doorway of our bedroom.

I sensed something very strange and unfamiliar in his voice. "Who is it?" I asked, looking up from my bent-over position on the edge of the bed. I was putting on my favorite "scamps," the casual shoes I like to wear with almost anything. He and I were about to go out to see a movie I had been dying to see.

"It's Johnny Wise's cousin," he said.

Johnny Wise was a friend of ours whom Darrell had met while they were both attending Fire Academy. They had finished training together. He and his wife, Annette, had become friends with us while he and Darrell underwent grueling training to become firefighters a few years ago.

Wondering what Johnny's cousin could possibly want with me, I screwed my face up into a question.

Darrell shrugged an answer back to me. "I think you need to talk to her," he said. He turned and walked back to Tjai's room where the phone was.

I got up and followed him. I sat down on Tjai's bed and picked up the telephone. Darrell sat across from me, on our two-year old son, Christopher's bed, the one he still hasn't slept in yet because we can't seem to get his little butt out of ours!

"Hello?"

The voice at the other end was a stranger to me. "Hello, Denise," the woman's voice said. "My name is Debra and you don't know me...yet, but you will." She paused.

"Okay," I said, waiting to hear more.

She continued. "Like I said, you don't know me yet, but..." again, she hesitated.

I waited.

Darrell looked at me and mouthed the words, "Who is she?"

I shrugged.

"Well," the voice went on, "I don't really know any other way to say this, but... well, I'm your sister."

"Okay," I said, nodding my head. After all, I had accumulated a lot of "sisters" about three years earlier when I became a member of the sisterhood of Delta Sigma Theta Sorority. Immediately, I presumed that Debra, too, was a member of the illustrious organization. Perhaps, I reasoned, she had gotten my number from another soror because she needed me for something. Maybe she needed a musician or vocalist for an upcoming wedding or something. I had played and sung for many affairs over the years and it was not uncommon for me to get calls like that. I didn't know what she needed, but since she told me that she was my "sister," I was all ears.

"No," she said, sensing that I had not really understood what she meant. "I'm your sister... your real sister." I didn't say anything. The words echoed in my head... 'Your sister... your real sister...'

"What is it?" Darrell asked, seeing a look on my face that he later described as total devastation.

I couldn't answer him. I was searching for something to say to the woman on the telephone. "What do you mean, my 'sister'?" I asked. I didn't wait for a response. "I have three brothers, but I don't have a sister."

"Yes, you do," she said. "I'm your sister." She sounded serious.

"But how?" I asked, incredulously. I had never heard anything about any "sister" before in my whole life. I could not imagine what on earth she could be talking about!

"We have the same father," Debra said.

I could sense that she was trying to break the news to me as gently as she could by the tone of this voice I was hearing for the very first time.

"Your mother's name was Almarine?" she asked.

"Yes."

"And your father's name was Samuel, right?"

I looked at Darrell.

He was staring at me.

That was one of the names I had been told he went by, so I just said, "yes." Funny, I didn't even know what my father's real name was. I guess I never cared enough about it to ask somebody, because I never did.

"Well, he was my father, too," she said.

33

My mind took off like a Seven-Forty-Seven! When could this have happened? How could this have happened? As soon as I asked myself that question, I knew it was a dumb one. I knew exactly how it could have happened. When and why were the questions I could not possibly answer! I didn't know it at that moment, but my "sister" was about to fill me in.

Again, she told me that her name was Debra, and she began by telling me how she had found me. She had seen a copy of the local newspaper that had contained the story about my decision to leave the school where I had been teaching as a result of student violence. The story began with a short introduction which detailed the night I had watched, at the age of eight, my father shoot and kill my mother, my maternal grandmother, wound my seven-year old brother, Michael, and my grandfather, before fatally turning the gun on himself. I had asked the reporter if he had really thought it necessary to mention the incident in the article concerning the school. I didn't think it was. He said that he thought it was very important, insisting that it would reveal my inner strength and determination to overcome a tragic childhood to become a teacher. To that end, the reporter, Mr. Wimbush, planned to mention that I had used the overcoming of my own tragic childhood experiences to inspire my students to rise above their own personal obstacles in life. I consented to the inclusion of the incident, but I did not want my picture in the newspaper. Mr. Wimbush again insisted, telling me that he thought it was very important to the article that I be photographed. I finally agreed to a picture with my husband, as we looked over some of the letters I had just received from numerous students at the school.

Debra's mother, Evelyn, had seen the article and the picture of Darrell and me. She painfully recollected that the man who had fathered her eldest daughter had been responsible for the horrible incident alluded to in the article. She looked at the accompanying photograph and instinctively, she knew she needed to contact her daughter, Debra. She knew that there could not possibly have been two tragic incidents like that in November of 1966! She called Debra over to her house and showed her the newspaper article. It just so happened that her nephew and our friend, Johnny Wise, was visiting her house at the time! Johnny took one look at the newspaper and told both Debra and Evelyn that he knew Darrell and me. It was through Johnny that Debra got my telephone number.

We talked for about fifteen minutes, unable to believe that after all of the time that had passed, we had arrived at that moment. She was elated, I could tell, about having finally found her sister. I was in shock! It was so hard to believe what Debra was saying to me! I had gotten used to the fact that I was the only girl and had grown up a "tomboy!" I played football with my brothers because it seemed like the thing to do. After all, they sure weren't going to play with dolls and there were never any "tea parties" at our house! I knew I couldn't beat them, so I just joined them! I played touch and tackle football with the other boys in the neighborhood, too! A sister?

In college, I remember not particularly wanting to share my personal things with my girlfriends because I had never had to share my things at home. I was the only girl! I had "girl" things! I never had to share with anyone in my house! My roommate and other girlfriends were always wearing each other's clothes and jewelry, using each other's cologne, and swapping nail polish. I once, reluctantly, managed to let someone borrow my Stevie Wonder's "Songs in the Key of Life" albums and I could hardly sleep a wink that night!

Now, here I was, talking to someone who claimed to be my sister! At once, I knew I had to see her! She wanted to see me, too! I asked her if I could come over to her house. Incredibly, she lived about five minutes away from us! Debra told me that she would love for me to come right over. She quickly gave me directions to her house.

Darrell and I piled our sons into our silver Lumina and rushed over to meet my "sister." On the way, I was thoughtfully quiet. A thousand and ten questions danced in my head! "Lord," I thought, "what is really going on?"

"What do you think?" my husband asked, sensing my uneasiness.

"I don't really know what to think," I said, "but when I see her, I'll know." I believed that once I looked into her eyes, saw her face, her smile, I would know if she indeed was my sister. Once I found out, I wasn't sure what I would do next!

In a very few minutes, we pulled up to the address Debra had given me. Two women were standing outside in front of a rickety little fence at the edge of a small yard. The grass was tall and brush-like. The two women watched as Darrell pulled the car up next to the fence and parked on the side of the house. The four of us got out of the car. I walked around, from the passenger side, to the front yard. When I had gotten within a couple of feet of the two women, I found myself staring in disbelief at the shorter of the two.

Almost immediately, I knew that this woman, whom I had never seen or heard of before that day, was my sister! I looked into her eyes and saw my own, staring back at me, under the dim light provided by a bulb on the front porch! She was darker than me, shorter and more slender than me, but she smiled... just... like... me! I was looking at my sister! The feeling I had was inexplicable! It was more than overwhelming! Her broad smile mirrored my own! I stood amazed! We embraced each other for a moment and then I introduced her to my husband, and our sons, Tjai and Christopher.

Debra introduced us to her friend, the other woman who had been standing in the yard with her. It felt very strange to hear her introduce me as her "sister." I knew that would take some getting used to! She invited us into the house and we followed her inside. I sat down on an earth-toned sofa in her living room, still unable to believe that I was sitting down with my father's other daughter! She began to tell me what she knew I was dying to know... how she came to be! I listened, a look of disbelief on my face, to Debra's story of how her mother, at the tender age of fourteen, was raped by a man she knew only as Samuel Clayton in 1957. At the time, my mother had been two months pregnant with me. I flooded her with questions she could not answer, but she graciously offered to call her mother, so that I could talk to her. Debra said that Evelyn could give me more information than she could.

In hushed tones, Debra and Darrell talked to each other while I spoke with Evelyn on the phone. She told me that my father had been a soldier, stationed at a nearby army base. That was the first time I had ever heard anything about that. I had never even known that he was in the army! She told me that she was just a teenager when she met my father. Her uncle had asked his army buddy, my father, to drive his fourteen year old niece home, as a favor to him. Instead, Samuel drove Evelyn out to a deserted area on the army reservation and did himself a favor! After the rape, he panicked, skipped town and was not heard of again until eight years later!

After I had spoken with Evelyn for a few minutes, I realized that my father, Samuel, Tony, James Earl Clayton, or whoever he really was, was even worse than I had previously imagined him to be! Only a monster would rape a fourteen year old girl, I thought! He was that monster! He was a horrible villain, a grue-some memory that I had locked away in a small room, deep within the farthest recesses of my mind. I had locked that monster up behind that door a long, long time ago. I thought that I would never, ever have to deal with him again. The pain he had given me was too enormous for me to think about, so I just didn't think about it. I didn't forget... I just didn't think about it any-more! It hurt too much! Even when I told the story of the agony and destruction Tony had brought into my life, I still didn't think about it as something that really happened. I just told the story.

As I sat and listened to Evelyn, my heart went out to her and Debra. My God! I thought. They had had their own share of tragedy! I found myself apologizing to Evelyn for what my father had done to her. She assured me that it wasn't my fault, but I still felt sorry for her having been violated by him. He had raped her!

He had taken from her a most valuable possession. I realized that Evelyn and I had a lot in common. She had hardly known him. Debra never knew him. She didn't know how fortunate she was to have never known him! As I ended my conversation with Evelyn, a warm tear ran down my cheek. There were so many emotions raging inside of me at that moment! I fought to maintain my composure as I hung up the phone and joined the conversation in progress between Debra and Darrell.

"You know," my husband observed, "you both hold your heads to the side in the same way when you're talking."

Debra giggled.

I smiled and consciously checked my body movements. I looked at her, sitting on the love seat across from me. She reminded me a lot of my - our - Aunt Martha, one of Tony's sisters who now lives in Omaha, Nebraska. I wondered if Aunt Martha, or anyone else on that side of the family, knew about Debra. If they did, they certainly kept that to themselves! I made a mental note to search for a picture I had at home. Aunt Martha was on it, along with some other Clayton family members. I had to find it! I needed to show it to Debra.

She had found me. Both of our lives now assumed added dimensions. As I looked at her across the room, I was convinced that that day had been coming since the beginning of creation. God evidently thought that its time had come!

I left Debra's house, feeling very strange, to say the least! I didn't quite know what to make of things! It was all so incredible to me! I went home and called my brothers, as well as other family members, to break the astonishing news to them. At first, no one believed me! Wayne, my oldest brother, laughed when I told him. He said that it was so incredible, it was plain funny! I had to agree with him.

The next morning, Darrell woke me up with a smile and asked, "So, how does it feel to have a sister?"

"I don't know," I said, stretching beneath the covers.

He was almost dressed to leave for work at the fire station. I watched him as he sat at the foot of the bed to put on his shoes. I still felt strange. All night long, I had dreamt about my father. It was very unpleasant. It was also very real! His face was blurred, but I knew it was him! I could hear his menacing voice as he spoke to me. "Well," the sultry voice said, "it's been a long time!" He was tall, dark and frightening! "Did you miss me?"

I was mortified! We were in a strangely ominous place. It was dark and empty, like infinite space and timelessness. Tony and me... together again! Unlike other times when I had fought to arouse myself to consciousness, away from the horror of my nightmares, I had not tried to wake up. For some reason I can't explain, I wanted to stay in the dream. I wanted the blurred vision to clear so that I could see Tony, for the first time in a long time. I don't know why I wanted so desperately to see him. Perhaps I was seeking verification of the features I had seen in Debra's face - features which definitely reminded me of him. I still had trouble believing she existed! One thing was certain though, she existed because of him.

Darrell sat down on the side of the bed and looked at me. As I returned his gaze, I thought about my dream, about Debra, and about the gigantic "mushroom" that had become the surging emotions now swelling inside of me. It had developed some time during the night. My abdomen was tight from the pressure. The feeling was like one people usually get after having eaten too much turkey and dressing on Thanksgiving Day. How well I knew that feeling!

I realized that meeting Debra meant much more than I could have ever bargained for! Seeing her familiar features brought Tony back to life for me! I had never intended to connect with him again, but she was the connection between him and me! He was back in my life, whether I wanted it or not! It was inevitable! Debra had no idea, but she was the key that unlocked the door I never intended to open again. She still doesn't know it, but before this is over, and perhaps when I get to know her better, I will probably tell her. Better yet, I think I will ask her to read the book.

I have since realized that the room where I kept Tony and other terrible memories of my past had grown rather crowded. After I tucked him safely away and locked the door, I learned to "reopen" it, only when necessary, to put other things, feelings, and experiences there, much like we have done with our attic. It is packed full of things we really could have just thrown away, but, for some reason or another, we put them up there with other "stuff." It is all stuff - stuff we don't want, stuff we don't need, stuff we'll never use again, stuff that should have gone straight to the dumpster! Instead, we kept it. We didn't feel like taking the time to sort through it, or we just didn't want to deal with it, so we put it up in the attic. There is a lot of stuff up there in that attic and I have a lot of "stuff" in that room. After a while, the space ran out and I locked it up and threw away the key. Amazingly, Debra had a duplicate! I believe God gave it to her. She didn't even know she had it, but He knew! With a simple sigh, he put into motion the series of events which brought the two of us together so that she could do something for me that I could not do for myself... unlock the door.

"Behold, I stand at the door and knock: if any man hear my voice, and open the door, I will come in to him, and will sup with him, and he with me." Rev. 3:30.

Two

During our early childhood, Wayne, Michael and I attended an elementary school near our house in Ft. Dodge, Iowa. Each day, we walked the distance from home to the red brick school building, each of us anxious about going to school! Some time in October of 1966, my mother, Almarine, suddenly appeared at the door of my third grade classroom. An anxious look on her pretty face, she whispered in my teacher's ear and the teacher instructed me to get my things because I was going to be leaving with my mother. I didn't really want to leave school, but I did as I was told. Out in the hallway, Wayne and Michael had already been summoned from their respective classrooms and were both waiting patiently for Mama and I.

"Come on," Mama said, "we have to go." She walked out of the school building, not even looking behind to see if we were following her.

"Go where?" I asked myself.

She stopped for a moment and turned around, as if sensing my bewilderment. I think she saw the question on my eight-year old face, but she didn't tell me or my brothers anything.

The next thing I remember, the five of us, Mama, my three brothers and I, were aboard a huge Greyhound bus, preparing to leave the small town of Fort Dodge. We rode for what seemed like an eternity to me. When we finally arrived in Columbus, Georgia, we were met at the bus station by my favorite aunt, Aunt Meg. She was my favorite because each time we came to Georgia, we always spent a lot of time with her and Uncle Harrison. They had no children of their own and had no reservations about spoiling us as much as any law would allow! I didn't know it then, but Aunt Meg later told me that shortly after our arrival, Mama told her that she was going to need her and Uncle Harrison to take care of us. At the time, Aunt Meg said, she didn't

41

know what Mama was talking about. When she asked her what she meant, Mama just asked her to promise that she would take care of the four of us and not let anyone split us up. Aunt Meg still didn't understand, but made the promise to Mama anyway.

Aunt Meg took us to our grandparents' house on Baldwin Street in an area known as "East Wynnton." The little house where Grandmama and Granddaddy lived was what people used to call a "shotgun house." They called it that because if you stood on the front porch, with the front and back doors open, you could see clear through to the back yard! I guess that meant that a person had a "clear shot" through the narrow, framed house. Several other shotgun houses sat up and down the streets of the predominantly black area of town.

I have no particular memory of the day we arrived in Columbus, but it was not very long before Mama had enrolled Wayne, Michael and me in an elementary school within walking distance of Grandmama's house. My aunt, Betty, lived just around the corner in a little apartment she shared with her three sons.

My mother told us that we were going to be staying with Grandmama and Granddaddy in their little shotgun house and already, I knew I liked the new living arrangements! As far as I knew, Tony was far, far away in Iowa and that suited me just fine! Easily, I settled in to living in Columbus. I loved my new school! I loved my new teacher! She was a petite Black woman named "Miss Patrick." She had a warm smile, and she was very affectionate towards me right from the start! Immediately, I set out to become her "pet!" She didn't necessarily have favorites, but she would let me bang the erasers to get the chalk dust out of them after class and that made me feel special! Isn't it peculiar that such insignificant things mean so much to children?

At the end of each day of the first week we went to school, Mama met us at the bottom of the hill and walked the rest of the way with us to Grandmama's house. On the way home, she asked us about our day. I would try to "out-talk" Wayne and Michael, telling her about the exciting things we had done — especially during recess! Wayne would roll his eyes upward as if he wished

I would just shut up, but seeing him do that just gave me "extra steam" and I would talk all the way home, nearly every day!

One day, I had stayed a little longer than usual, cleaning Miss Patrick's erasers. When I finally trekked across the playground, heading for the street, I looked up saw Mama, walking towards me. She looked nervous and extremely upset. I looked around for Wayne and Michael, but I didn't see them. I eagerly searched Mama's face.

"Your daddy's here," she whispered, although no one was close enough to hear. She reached for me. Her hand was damp with perspiration.

I didn't say anything, but I was very disappointed to hear that Tony had come to Columbus! Things had been going so well without him around. Mama had been so much happier. She smiled much more. Ronnie had stopped all that screaming he had been so prone to do back in Iowa. Even I was more at ease because there was no fussing, no fighting, no cursing, no yelling, and definitely no "Daddy-beating-up-on-Mama-again" in Columbus! If he had come to live with us, I knew that our peace was about to come to a screeching halt!

Mama rushed me down the hill towards Grandmama's house. Wayne and Michael had walked on ahead, but we caught up with them quickly. From the sorrowful expressions on their faces, I could tell that they had already heard the bad news. No one said anything all the way home this time — including me! When we reached the house, I kept looking around, looking for him, but apparently, he was not there. We all went inside.

Later that evening, Tony showed up. He acted as if he was overjoyed to see us, holding me so tightly, I could hardly breathe! I was as stiff as a board in his arms. I peered around him at my brothers. Similar looks of disappointment showed on their faces.

That night, Wayne, Michael and I sat on the floor in the "front room," my grandmother's living room, near the screened door, and listened, as Tony made promises to Mama which we had all heard many times before. They were sitting, side-by-side, in Grandmama's old porch swing. As the swing rocked gently back and forth, he told her that he had been upset that she had taken us and left the way she did. But, he assured Mama, none of that mattered now. What mattered was that we were together again. He wanted us to be a family, he said, a real family! He said that he was going to look for a job and take care of us like a good man was supposed to take care of his family. If Mama preferred Columbus to Fort Dodge, Tony said, we could all just stay there! He was going to show her that he was a good man. He would show her if she would just give him one more chance!

Just one more chance… how many times had we heard that before? We looked at each other, almost afraid to breathe, wondering if Mama would take him back again and give him another chance to hurt her and to hurt us by hurting her.

Neither of us could hear what her answer was, but Tony seemed to be enthused by it. They both stood up. Excitedly, he swooped her up off of the concrete porch and hugged her tightly. He told her that he would come and pick her up on Friday so that they could go out on the town to "celebrate!" Tony left and Mama approached the door to come inside the house. We scampered quickly away from the door. I remember looking into Mama's face and noticing that she didn't look as happy as Tony had. In fact, she actually looked miserable!

The incident which I am about to describe is one that I have spoken about on a few selective occasions. I shared some of it during a testimonial service at church once. I had been thinking about how good God had been to me in my lifetime, even when bad things seem to happen to me or to those whom I loved. I have even shared the tragic details of the incident with some of my students at school, in an effort to show them that despite childhood tragedies or obstacles in life, you can still go on to achieve great things! I felt that what I had chosen to do, or rather, what God had led me to do, in becoming a teacher, was a great accomplishment — particularly for someone who had had such a devastating childhood! I told my students that if I could rise above my own tragic circumstances, they, too, could rise above theirs! I talked to them about the man who was my "father" and the terrible things he did. I thought that by talking about it, I was actually dealing with my experiences. I wasn't! I realize that, although I talked about "I" and "me" and "us" and "we," in first person, I was actually talking about my life's experiences in third person.

I created an "aesthetic distance" between my real life and the person I became. Aesthetic distances allow us to step back or away from the picture in order to see the "beauty" of it. That's exactly what I did. I wanted to see the beauty instead of the ugly horror that my life had been! So I testified about the tragic childhood of the little girl who was me. I reported the facts as if I was doing the six o'clock news and I was as objective as any good news reporter was expected to be.

On Friday, sure as the sun was shining, Tony showed up to fulfill his promise. He sauntered in and swooped me up in his arms. His smile seemed wider and brighter than usual. He hugged me hard and then set me down on the floor in front of him. He reached into his shirt pocket and took out a letter. As he handed the letter to me, his other hand went into his pants pocket. From it, he extracted a jewelry box, something else for me. I was surprised because I could not ever remember him giving me anything. Like any other curious child, I wanted to see what was in the box first! I opened it and my mouth dropped open when I saw its contents. Inside was a watch, but not a child's watch. It was a woman's watch with a white face, surrounded by tiny, sparkling diamonds. The band was a black, doubled elastic rope. It was very pretty, but I couldn't figure out why he was giving it to me. At the age of eight, I couldn't tell time very well, but surely, this was too grown-up for me. Even I knew that! The elegant watch hung from my fingers as I opened the letter. Tony grinned proudly as he watched me begin to read it silently.

"Read it out loud," he said. He often liked to hear me read aloud. He used to say that I was so smart that I was going to be "a real genius some day!" In his doting manner, he encouraged me to demonstrate my developing "smarts" at each and every opportunity.

I didn't really feel like being a genius right then, but I knew he wouldn't let me off the hook, so I began to read. I read aloud the letter he had taken obvious pains to write to me, but I swear I cannot remember one single, solitary word of it. I do know, however, that when he wrote it, his intentions were to let me know how much he loved me. He said that he had planned to mail it to me, but when he decided to come to Columbus, he thought it would be better if he brought it to me and delivered it personally. I later learned that Tony had "borrowed" his brother's car on the pretense of going to the store to buy cigarettes. The store he wanted to go to just happened to be hundreds and hundreds of miles away from Fort Dodge, in Columbus, Georgia. That's how he had happened to "show up" unannounced at Grandmama's house!

When I had finished my task, Tony smiled gleefully and gave me another tight squeeze. In a matter of minutes, his smile had quickly turned to a frown. Much to Tony's dismay, Mama had changed her mind. She did not want to go out with him after all. Boy, was he ticked off! The calm, loving demeanor he had shown me just moments earlier quickly dissipated and was replaced by the ravenous anger I knew only too well! He yelled at Mama that he had plans and he was not going to let her screw them up! Mama insisted that she simply did not want to go but suggested that she might feel like going the following night.

Tony refused to take "no" for an answer. Forcefully, he grabbed her and despite my grandparents' protests, tried to drag Mama towards the front door.

Michael and I rushed to her rescue, yelling for Tony to "Stop!" and "Leave her alone!" We pounded on his strong, dark arms to release her. Had Wayne been there, he, too, would have done everything in his power to make Tony leave our mother alone! Earlier that afternoon, she had given him permission to spend the night around the street, at Aunt Betty's house. He had been dying to spend some time with her son, Eric, who was just a few years older than he. Little did he know, when he left for Aunt Betty' house that afternoon, that he would never see Mama alive again!

46

It seemed that Tony had gone to a world all his own and he was trying to drag Mama into it with him — away from the house and away from us! It was clear to us that she had no desire to go with him. We didn't want her to go either! Michael and I pounded on his arms as hard as we could! Suddenly, Tony turned his head and looked down at me. He had a peculiar expression on his face, as if he had just come back to reality. I guess he was stunned. He seemed unable to believe that I, his little girl, the one he loved so much, could be against him. He never knew it, but I had never been for him!

Tony released Mama, his strong arms dropping to his sides. He looked at me through glassy eyes. For a brief second, I thought he was going to cry. Then, quite abruptly, he turned and stormed out of the house! Mama rushed to the door and locked it behind him. It seemed to me that there were at least three locks on the door. I remember hearing them click, the last one, a deadbolt, loud and empty-sounding.

The next sequence of events, unfortunately, are more clear in my mind now than ever. It seemed like things were going to settle down. Tony was gone, or so we thought, and Mama was still there with us. I was hoping that he would go on off and find something else to do and someone else to do it with! Mama seemed relieved that the excitement was over and told us that it was time for us to get ready for bed.

Michael always seemed to be the first one to go. He slept on a cot that had been set up for him next to the window in Grandmama's and Granddaddy's room, in the middle of the house. He had already gone and climbed into bed. I could see the top of his small, curly head resting innocently on his pillow.

Mama pulled the sofa bed out to its full length and covered it with fresh, crisp sheets and top covers so that Ronnie and I could get into bed. We had been sleeping there since our arrival in Columbus — Mama, Ronnie and I. After she had completed her task, I sat down at the foot of the sofa bed. Ronnie, who was only three years at the time, stood next to me, one chubby little hand resting on my knee. He was as fascinated as I was with a lady on the television set in one corner of the room. She was belting out a song which I had never heard before. We stared at her, listening intently. I didn't know the name of the song she was singing, but I would never be able to forget one of the next songs that would ring out into every crevice of that little shotgun house.

Grandmama had gone into her room, the same room where Michael had just drifted off to sleep. I don't know where my grandfather was at the exact moment the thunderous banging at the front door began. It was louder than anything I had ever heard! It was like cannons, exploding in the night! It was frightening, loud and full of anger! It was Tony! I could not see him through the heavy wooden door, but I knew it was him. Anxiously, I looked at my mother and her face had turned white! Grandmama appeared in the doorway and shouted, "Almarine, call the police!" Her voice sounded strangely hollow to me, like she was far away. I looked at her. She was standing within a few feet of me.

A sudden movement registered in the corner of my eye and I spun around to see Ronnie, starting towards the door. I watched him, my mouth open wide. He was moving in slow motion, his tiny body wobbling, gravitating towards the tremendous sound! In a moment of panic, I sprang up from the sofa bed and rushed to him. I grasped his tiny hand in mine and literally yanked him backwards, away from the door. "No!" I whispered, desperately.

Somewhere in the midst of the confusion, Granddaddy had gone to his room to get one of his guns. He kept everything locked up! Everything! He was very busy, fumbling, trying to get the key in the lock on the large trunk which sat ominously in one corner of the bedroom, near an antique dresser. He tugged at the lock fiercely, but it simply would not budge!

Amazingly, Michael had not stirred amidst the terrible banging on the front door! The top of his head was still visible on the fluffy, white pillow. I couldn't believe he hadn't gotten up! I have wished a thousand times since that Michael had gotten up! I wished that the banging had snatched him from his dreams so that he could have jumped up out of his slumber and perhaps into safety! But it didn't! He didn't move!

Just as suddenly as the awful noise began, it stopped! Just like that! It stopped! My eyes sought Mama's through the deafening silence. She looked back at me. She was holding the telephone receiver in her hand. She had been talking to someone on the other end. Now, she was silent. Her face was wet with a mixture of tears and sweat. I stared at her. I couldn't understand what was happening. She said something into the mouthpiece. I couldn't make out what she was saying, but I really looked at her. I'm glad I did because that was the last time I would really have the opportunity to see my mother's beautiful face.

Before anyone realized what was going on, the real noise began. It was a sound I would never want to hear again in life! That sound was gunfire! Tony was shooting through the window in my grandparents' room. Mama was in that room, still holding the receiver! Granddaddy was in that same room, still fumbling with the lock on his trunk! In that same room, Michael was sleeping on the cot near the window! Now Tony was shooting through that very same window!

Almost instantly, Michael sprang up out of the cot, screaming like a wounded animal! His voice was small, but his cry filled my head. I stood in the doorway, unable to believe my eyes! Mama dropped the receiver. My eyes followed it as it bounced on the hardwood floor!

Granddaddy finally got the lock off of the trunk and was fumbling with his Winchester. He was trying to load it. His hands shook violently!

I ran to Michael! Mama and I lifted him up and carried him to the sofa bed. He was bleeding profusely! His blood stained my pajamas. I searched Mama's face for some explanation. What was happening? Why was this happening? What was Tony trying to do? Going to do? Why did he hurt Michael? Mama was crying, cradling her middle son in her arms. She rocked him gently as tears rolled down her cheeks. I realized that I was crying, too.

Grandmama appeared in the doorway. I remember wondering where she had been. Granddaddy rushed past her and yelled something incoherent. I turned around and looked at

49

three-year old Ronnie. He was standing in front of the television, looking from the blurry screen and back to the incredible chaos around him! He didn't seem to know what was going on. Someone on the television was singing. I have never been able to forget that song, "What the World Needs Now is Love, Sweet Love." For some strange reason, I stopped and listened to the woman singing. I don't know why I stopped, in the midst of my world being completely shattered, and listened to that lady sing "No, not just for some, but for everyone," she sang. Love? Was this love?

Abruptly, the shooting through the window ceased. The white sheers had dark powdery holes in them. The sheets on the cot were smeared with Michael's blood. The mouth of the trunk gaped open, as if waiting for something. Mama carefully laid Michael down on the sofa bed in the living room and rushed back to the phone. She snatched it up off the floor and started screaming into the mouthpiece. I went completely deaf! I saw her lips moving, but I couldn't hear a word she said.

Grandmama was standing in front of the mantle in the living room. I noticed a can of DeVoe snuff on the shelf behind her. She had some in her mouth, too. A bulge poked out beneath her bottom lip. I ran to Grandmama and threw my arms around her waist. She gently stroked my back. I knew she could feel my heart pounding because it permeated my entire body! Ronnie was now staring at us, a puzzled expression on his face. The woman on television was singing her heart out, I knew, but there was nothing else she could say to me.

My hearing was restored when I heard glass breaking in the kitchen and Grandmama's pantry shelves crashing to the floor! Grandmama and I peered around the doorway to see what was happening. The sight was horrendous! Tony was a huge, dark, venomous creature, a monster covered with White Lily flour from head to toe! In his hand was a revolver, black and threatening, as he crept slowly through the house. Mama was still there, holding the phone. They were in the same room! Once, Tony shot her in the leg and she fell down to the floor, still grasping the receiver. Her blood splattered on the wall! The black, wire phone stand fell over on the floor beside her.

Granddaddy was at the front door now, shooting at Tony! They exchanged rapid gunfire between them!

Michael lay bleeding on the sofa bed. I wanted to go to him, but I was afraid to move!

Somehow, Grandmama and I had managed to get right in the line of fire, between Tony and Granddaddy! I looked up into her eyes, those eyes that had scolded me, tickled me, laughed at me, and cried with me. Her eyes were saying something to me which I could not comprehend. The only sound in my ears was the rat-tat-tat of the black, shining pistol in Tony's hand and Granddaddy's shotgun blasting!

I finally managed to speak. "He's going to kill all of us!" I cried. It was more of a question. I needed some kind of reassurance.

Then my grandmother said the strangest thing to me. What was even more strange was that she almost smiled as she said it. "No, baby, he's not going to kill you. Your daddy loves you."

At that moment, I glared at her, wondering if she had gone insane! In the next, Grandmama was falling! Down, down, she fell to the floor at my feet! I stared down at her! She had been shot! But how? I didn't understand how that could have happened. I looked down at myself. Was I shot, too? There was blood on my pajamas! Then I remembered Michael, lying on the sofa bed. I turned to look at him. He appeared to be asleep. The blood on my pajamas was his, not mine! It was his!

Suddenly, I noticed Ronnie. He had come to stand a few feet away from me. He was looking down at Grandmama, too. She was still moving on the floor.

Something swept over me! I don't know what it was! Some unseen force moved my legs, my arms, my body over to where Ronnie was. Then, I did something that I didn't understand. I grabbed him and pulled him down to the floor. I knelt down and pushed my little brother as far as I could underneath the sofa bed. "Hurry!" I whispered anxiously to him. Obediently, he scooted his tiny little body over, keeping his brown eyes focused on me.

I laid down on my stomach and followed him under the bed. We slid directly underneath Michael, who lay sleeping on top of the bed. I tried to maneuver my own body over, on top of Ronnie's. I didn't want him to get shot, too! I thought that if I covered him and Tony shot underneath the bed, he might kill me, but Ronnie would be protected from the gunfire. I was willing to die for him! He was just a baby! I felt his warm body beneath my own. Ronnie clung to me. He never made a sound!

I kept my eyes wide open. I wanted to see Tony when he knelt down and looked under that bed for me! I wasn't ready to die, but I wanted to be able to look into his eyes when he took my life! He had already destroyed it! I knew that life could never be the same again! I waited, but he never came for me.

The shooting stopped. I didn't know it then, but Granddaddy had been hit! Somehow, he had been knocked out of the door, onto the front porch! I hadn't even realized that the front door was open! I listened and I could hear the muffled sounds of Tony and Mama, talking to each other in the next room.

"Tony, please!" she cried. "Don't do this! You don't have to do this!" Her voice itself was a plea. It was soft and murmuring, like a gentle wind.

I imagine that when Satan speaks, he sounds just like Tony sounded when he answered her. "I told you," he snarled, "if I can't have you, nobody else will!" And with those words, I heard another shot!

Silence.

I waited. I strained my ears to hear Mama's voice again. I didn't know what was going on! I wanted to know! I wanted to know what Tony was doing to her! I remember thinking that maybe I should crawl out from my hiding place to go and see, but I didn't want Ronnie to follow me and I believed that if I moved, he would. He was clinging to me just like he usually clung to Mama.

The other day, I was looking at a picture of them... Mama holding Aunt Tisa's baby, Wimp, and Ronnie, clinging to Mama's leg. He was always clinging to her. I stayed where I was, under the sofa bed, and let him cling to me.

I heard another shot! I flinched. There was a curious thud on the floor! Everything was still and quiet. All of a sudden, I heard the television set. The audience was applauding wildly! About what, I didn't know. But why they would be applauding, I wondered. I remember thinking that they were stupid and that the show was stupid, too. But the most ridiculous thing of all was that stupid song about love!

"Nesi?"

I started, hearing Granddaddy's raspy voice calling to me from out on the front porch. The door was flung open wide. I was afraid to answer because I knew that if I did, Tony would probably hear me and he would know where I was. I believed that he would come and kneel down and shoot me, right between the eyes! I was frozen still!

Granddaddy called to me again, "Nesi? Nesi, you hear me?" He coughed.

I gathered up the nerve to answer. Tony would just have to find me out. "Huh?" I said, audibly.

"Come on out here," Granddaddy said.

"I can't," I responded, my voice trembling.

"Yes, you can," he said. "Come on, now!" He coughed again.

I inhaled as much air as I could and breathed it out quickly. My chest ached. "He's going to kill me," I whispered loud enough for him to hear.

"No," Granddaddy assured me. "No, he's not… He's dead."

Dead? Dead? How could he be dead? What happened? I felt as if I were dreaming. Tony, dead? No, he couldn't be! People like him don't die! Good people die, I thought. Bad people live on and on so they can torment the rest of us forever!

"Be sober, be vigilant; because your adversary the devil, as a roaring lion, walketh about, seeking whom he may devour." 1 Peter 5:8

I remember having a discussion once, with my cousin Elaine. We were both seven years old, living in Fort Dodge. We were sitting on our grandmother's front porch steps, talking about a lady who had lived down the street from us. She had recently died. She had been very nice to us. She used to let us climb up in her apple tree and pick sweet, green apples out of it. She would tell us to "just get one" so we wouldn't get a stomach ache. We would usually slip one in each of our pockets when she wasn't looking and come down from the billowy tree with one big, shiny, sweet green apple in our small hands and angelic smiles on our motley faces. That kind old woman died. She was a good person. After she died, Elaine and I were both sad and confused. We went to our grandmother to ask her why that nice old lady had to die.

Grandma Tiny tried to console us by telling us that God always took the good folks on home because He wanted them up in Heaven with Him. "Anyway," she told us, "they deserved to go on home, away from the troubles of this old world."

Why, I wondered, didn't old Satan collect himself a few of the bad ones and take them on to hell so there wouldn't be so much trouble in this old world? That was the first time I questioned God's motives. The second time occurred when one of my cousins' newborn baby died. I didn't even know the beautiful, doll-like infant's name. I remember us all going to the funeral home to see her, sleeping peacefully in a miniature casket. She looked just like an angel! Elaine and her sisters, Shirley, Carolyn, Helen, and I stood close to the open casket and gazed down at the tiny baby. She had been just a few weeks old when she died. I didn't understand it. I had planned to ask Grandma Tiny why the baby died, but I never got a chance to.

Somebody in the family viewing room passed gas, all the kids busted out laughing, and poor Grandma Tiny was so embarrassed, she rushed us all out of the room and made us go and sit in the car! On the way home, she was so mad, she told us that she would tar and feather anyone who so much as breathed loud enough for her to hear them! I knew it would not be a good time to ask about the baby. In the weeks that followed, her mood didn't seem to get any better. By the time it did, I had forgotten the question.

"Who will render to every man according to his deeds."
Rom. 2:6

"Come on, baby," Granddaddy said. His voice was becoming weaker.

I took another deep breath and pushed myself out from underneath the bed. Grandmama was crawling on the floor! My eyes widened at a puddle of blood that had formed beneath her! Her lips were moving. She still had snuff under her tongue. Brown liquid ran down one side of her chin. I looked at Michael. He had begun to stir in his sleep, making a strange, gurgling noise. He groaned in pain. I knew that he was badly hurt!

I needed to see Mama! I needed to know that she was all right! There were no sounds coming from the middle room. I wanted to see her! I wanted to see Tony to make sure he was dead like Granddaddy had said! I cautiously stepped over Grandmama on the floor. She was making a deep moaning sound now. I tiptoed to the doorway and was shocked beyond belief at the scene that met me! Mama was lying on the floor, her hazel eyes staring up at the ceiling! One side of her face was bloody and part of her head appeared to be missing! Her full lips were still crimson with her favorite lipstick, but her red lips were still. One look told me that she was dead! Her eyes were open, but I knew my mother was dead! My heart flip-flopped in my chest! I put my hands over it to make it stop, but the pounding seemed to get worse!

Tony was lying across her, their bodies forming a crucifix! I couldn't see his face, not that I wanted to. In fact, I knew that I didn't ever want to see his face again! I became very angry! He had torn my whole world apart! He had taken from me the one thing I loved most...Mama! I looked at his long body on the floor through the tears, forming in my eyes. The hatred I had already felt for him grew by leaps and bounds as I glowered at him! He had said that he loved me, but it was a lie! It was all an awful lie! How could he have said that he loved me when he had taken my love away from me? I don't think he really knew what love was!

55

Granddaddy called to me again and I remembered him out on the front porch. I turned and ran through the living room, outside to him! I found him lying in the porch swing, one leg dangling curiously from it.

"Go next door," he ordered me. "Tell Mrs. Bee to call the police!"

I turned my head and looked up the street, astonished to see the flashing blue lights of a police squad car, parked just two houses up front us. The car sat in front of the house on the corner. How long had they been there? I wondered. They were two houses - two shotgun houses - up the street from us! Surely, they had heard all of the shooting! All of the noise! What on earth had they thought it was? Fireworks? In November? Why were they up there instead of here, saving my mother's life? Anger engulfed me!

"Go!" Granddaddy commanded, with all of the strength he had left.

I hurdled over the three steps off the porch into the yard and ran out of the gate, over to Mrs. Bee's house, next door. I banged on the door so hard, my hand hurt. Quickly, the porch light came on and the door opened.

"What—?" the elderly woman began.

I didn't wait for her to finish the question. "Mrs. Bee! Please call the police" I screamed. "My mama's dead!"

"Nesi?" she began, opening the screen door to me. "Baby, what happened?"

"Please," I begged, "please call the police!" My whole body shook uncontrollably.

She pulled me into the house with her. When she saw the blood, Michael's blood, on my pajamas, she cried, "Oh my God!" Mrs. Bee pulled me to her.

I collapsed in her arms.

"Fathers, provoke not your children to anger, lest they be discouraged." Colossians 3:21

Just remembering that awful night brought every emotion and fear I had then to my present. While writing the words which described my most painful experience, I had to stop several times just to calm the pounding of my heart and allow my breathing to return to normal. I found myself stopping, wringing my hands, trying to absorb the shock which accompanied the turbulent memory. At one point, I stopped and left my seat at the computer and began to fold some clothes that had been waiting days to be put away. Since I began writing, I had been almost single-minded, unable to think about very much else! Each memory seemed to trigger yet another... and another. It was all very frightening to me.

The other day, I said to my sister, Debra, that somehow, I believe we were together at our respective births, in some spiritual way. I don't know if she understood what I meant. She just nodded. I also told her that I believe God let us go our separate ways, without any knowledge of each other, in order that we go full circle in our individual lives. There must have been some reason we had to wait thirty-eight years to find each other. It is a mysterious situation — but then, God does move in a mighty mysterious way! Our finding each other, or rather, Debra's finding me, is quite another amazing act of God!

I didn't tell her all the details about Tony's murdering rampage. I told her that 'yes, it did happen' and 'yes, it changed my life forever!' Ironically, she told me that she only recalled seeing Tony once in her entire life. Earlier that day, before we all came face-to-face with the destiny he had chosen for us, he stopped by to see Debra and her mother, Evelyn. Debra told me that her grandmother told her that he was her father. Tony gave her three dollars, the only thing he had ever given to her. He had tried to take Evelyn off, away from her home, but her mother would not allow him to. Like Debra, I, too, wondered if he had had a similar fate planned for Evelyn. I guess we'll never know the answer to that question.

Afterwards, Debra's grandmother told her of the horrible crime her father had committed. She told me that she had assumed that Tony had killed everyone in the house. That is why she was so stunned to learn that my brothers and I were still alive! She had been out in the yard playing when her grandmother called her inside to tell her about her father. After she received the news that he had killed the occupants of the house on Baldwin Street and then killed himself, the tiny eight year old girl went back outside to play, little affected by the news of the death of a man she never knew.

My pastor, Rev. Thompson, told me once that God had gifted me with a compassionate spirit. Throughout my life, I have almost instinctively tried to protect those whom I love. I didn't realize that until Darrell and I had a counseling session with Pastor Thompson. We seemed to be in the midst of a struggle, not uncommon for two married people. A conflict occurred because of differences in our childrearing methods — methods we have individually developed from our own separate backgrounds and experiences. Oh yes, this all makes perfect sense to me now, after having talked it through! I thank God for the spiritual guidance he has given us in our pastor, Rev. Thompson! My own stubbornness and ignorance could have cost me my husband — the one I am absolutely sure God sent to me!

Unfortunately, my instinct to protect is most likely the result of that tragic night in November when I lost my mother. I can no longer talk about it in "third person." I can no longer just report the facts. The fact of the matter is that the horrible life-shattering incident didn't happen "around" me. It happened "to" me!

God, in His infinite wisdom, has seen fit to bring me to a point in my life where I have no choice other than to take a good, hard look at that story and see it for what it truly is — mine! Finding my sister has brought back to my remembrance, a lot of emotions which I thought I would never be capable of handling. However, God must have had a little more faith in me than I had in myself, because He allowed Debra and I to find each other. He permitted me to take a look behind the door that had been closed and barred in the depths of my mind for at least thirty years now. Finding Debra not only meant finding a sister, but also reopening old wounds, the memories I have of my father — extremely painful memories!

"I know thy works: behold, I have set before thee an open door, and no man can shut it: or thou has a little strength, and hast kept my word, and has not denied my name." Rev. 3:8

To say that I hated my father is too kind, but for lack of a better word, at this point, I can honestly say that I hated the man! Even when he kissed my face and uttered empty words of love to me, I hated him! When he hit my mother, I hated him. Even when he didn't hit her, I still hated him! But my hatred reached new heights when he did more to hurt me than he could ever have done, whether that was or was not his intention. He took my mother away from me. As far as I am concerned, killing himself was the easy way out. He didn't want to have to face anyone or suffer any consequences for the awful sins he had committed. I don't think he realized it, but death was no escape! He will still have to answer to God for the things he did. When I began writing, I still had one regret. I would never be able to face him to tell him just what he did to me!

Later that awful night, after some of the excitement had died down and reality began to sink in, Ronnie and I joined Wayne at Aunt Betty's house. After the hoards of people left, we settled down to try to get some sleep.

Wayne had already gone to bed in the room with our cousin, Eric. I didn't know whether he was sleeping or not, but I could not close my eyes. I had already seen too much and I was scared to death of what the darkness might show me! Aunt Betty had prepared her sofa bed in the living room for Ronnie and I to sleep on. The sofa bed sat in front of a large picture window. With a mental vision of what had happened to Michael just a few hours earlier still fresh on my mind, I had already decided that I could not sleep near the window! I could not get my mind off of him, sleeping peacefully next to the window. I kept seeing his little head resting on the pillow and then his fragile body being catapulted out of the bed, blood pouring from his wounds! In my head, I could still hear him screaming in agony! I sat up, trembling. Ronnie sat up, too.

Aunt Betty was still up and about. She had been crying off and on about Mama and Grandmama. She walked into the living room to find Ronnie and I sitting up on the sofa bed. "What's the matter?" she asked, her voice hoarse. She sat down on the sofa bed next to me.

"I can't go to sleep," I said.

She hugged me. "Everything's going to be all right."

I knew that she was lying. How could anything ever be all right again?

"Ronnie," she said to my little brother, "lie down and go to sleep, baby."

Then Ronnie said something that I would never be able to forget, as long as I live. In his small, soft, baby voice, he said, "I want Rengie." That was what he had called Mama, Rengie.

I began to cry fresh tears. I put my arms around him. "I'll take care of you," I whispered, hugging him. "I'll take care of you from now on." In the years to come, I would find myself trying to do just that, at all costs!

Three

After the joint funeral services for Mama and Grandmama, it was decided that Aunt Meg and Uncle Harrison would take the four of us — well, if Michael survived, there would still be four of us. He was still in the hospital's Intensive Care Unit. No one really expected him to make it. Wayne, Ronnie, and I had already been moved into the little frame house on Twenty-Second Street. Since our newly acquired parents had never before had any children of their own, their modest home was not readily equipped for four kids at once! A lot of modifications had to be made. The den was rapidly converted into a bedroom.

Aunt Meg already had a sofa bed. Wayne and Ronnie were to sleep there. She soon purchased a set of bunk beds. I slept on top and if and when Michael came home from the hospital, he would sleep on the bottom.

No one discussed what had happened to our family. It was "taboo" to mention Tony or the devastation he had caused us. Any and all pictures of him were promptly and utterly destroyed. He no longer existed to us. He was no longer a part of our family. He was dead and gone, but only I know where he had taken up residence. Subconsciously, I had put him there. My world became very quiet, very still. There was not much left for me. I had Wayne and Ronnie, but in my own mind, Michael was almost gone, too. No one spoke of him. We truly believed that Michael had died that night, too! I did not even wonder why his casket had not been set in the church between Mama's and Grandmama's. I took for granted that his death had been far too overwhelming for anyone to deal with in the midst of the great loss we had already suffered. If Michael had died, I was sure that he had gone to Heaven. He had probably seen the lady with apple tree and the tiny doll-like baby there. I wondered if he was happy; I hoped that he was. I sure wasn't!

Wayne seemed to put all of his energy into playing ball. If it wasn't football, it was baseball or basketball. It was always some kind of ball! Sports probably got him through the loss he, too, had suffered.

Ronnie didn't seem very much affected by his new environment. He simply went from calling Mama "Mama," to calling Aunt Meg "Mama." She was the one who clothed and fed him, hugged and kissed him, scolded and spanked him. For all intents and purposes, she was "Mama" now. He clung to her just like he had clung to his "Rengie."

I felt very much betrayed and alone! I could not deal with my sadness because I was too consumed with being angry with Tony! Each day, I prayed that he was somewhere suffering excruciatingly for what he had done! Wherever hell was, I was sure that he had found it. I only hoped that he would be tormented forever. In my heart, I already knew that I would be.

My world was too quiet without Mama. I began to notice things I had never really paid much attention to before... clocks ticking, floors creaking, and people breathing around me, as we stared at the television set in Aunt Meg's bedroom. Cool air sloshed through my ears and my own heartbeat pounded in my head. I needed something, but I didn't know what! I desperately needed something to fill the increasing emptiness inside of me. I began to look for something big enough to plug the enormous hole in my heart.

Aunt Meg had been taking piano lessons from a man everyone in town called "Smokey." He lived in East Wynnton. He was a well-known musician in town, and he taught music in the tiny living room of his little shotgun house, which happened to be right down the street from the house where Mama and Grandmama had died! Aunt Meg's music book sat on the piano in our living room. Every time I passed it, I glanced at it, but I would not dare touch it! It was her personal book and somehow seemed "sacred" to me. I sat and listened from another room in the house as she practiced almost every day. She used to play "Swans on the Lake," and I listened intently as she played, somewhat awkwardly, missing notes here and there. I closed my eyes and began to memorize the sounds emanating from the upright Cote. After a while, when Aunt Meg would leave me home alone on errands to the store or elsewhere, I began to go into the living room, sit down at the piano, turn to "Swans on the Lake" and play what I had heard her play.

Over and over, I played. I closed my eyes and let my fingers glide across the keys. The sound floated up out of the instrument, filling my ears and reaching my heart. I had found something! It wasn't Mama, of course, but it was something! It could never take her place, but still, it was something!

I couldn't read the little round notes. I just played, my fingers mimicking what I had heard Aunt Meg play, No one knew I could play the piano, no one but God. He knew because it was a gift He had given to me! He gave it to me because He knew I needed something! That's how God is. He always gives us what we need. I didn't know that then, but I know it now. I began to play whenever I found myself in the house alone. When I was sure that everyone was gone, I rushed to the piano, sat down and played to my heart's content. I began to turn on the radio and pick out the melody of whatever song was playing. Before long, I could play just about anything I heard! I played "by ear" people would later observe when my secret was out. That's what folks said about musicians who did not read music, but could play as if they could. I became one of them.

One day, Aunt Meg left the house on an errand to the grocery store. She was preparing food for a huge wedding reception for which she was catering. She had left me alone at the house. My brothers were outside, playing, as usual. After I was certain she had gone, I went to the piano, sat down and began to play "Lightly Row," another song Aunt Meg had been practicing. Unbeknownst to me, she had left her grocery list on the kitchen counter. When she discovered her error, Aunt Meg stopped the car a few houses up the street, turned around and came back to retrieve her list. When she walked in on me playing the piano, she stopped dead in her tracks.

"When did you learn to do that?" she asked, unable to believe what her ears had heard.

Abruptly, I stopped and turned around on the bench to face her. I shrugged my shoulders. "I don't know," I murmured, matter-of-factly.

Aunt Meg smiled, obviously happy with her new discovery. "You're going to take piano lessons!" she said, enthusiastically. "I didn't know you could play like that!" She was ecstatic. You're the one who should be taking lessons, not me!"

I wasn't sure that I wanted to take piano lessons. I knew I would have to talk to someone, a piano teacher, and I wasn't ready to talk to anyone. Aunt Meg was ready for me. She was anxious for me to meet Smokey and she quickly arranged for my lessons to commence!

At first, she drove me to my lessons twice a week. Later on, I rode the bus to Mr. Mathis' house on Baldwin Street. As the huge bus passed my grandmother's empty house, a twinge in my chest reminded me of the hole in my heart. At Mr. Mathis' house, I would temporarily forget about it. At Mr. Mathis' house, there was music! As the weeks and months went by, each time I passed Grandmama's house, I turned my head so that I wouldn't have to look at it anymore.

A short time after Aunt Meg discovered my musical abilities, Michael came home. A couple of weeks before, he had been given up for dead! The doctors had abandoned any hopes of his recovery from the injuries he had sustained that fateful night. Several gunshots had punctured his scrawny body. A long diagonal scar crossed his torso and there were tiny scars where the bullets had entered his body. The doctors had given up on him! They had, as I have often heard ministers say, "turned their backs and walked away." God stepped in and performed a miracle on Michael! He spared his young life! God showed us all that He was still in control!

The day that everyone, except God, gave up on Michael, the doctors suggested to Aunt Meg that she bring us up to the hospital so that we could say "good-bye" to him from the parking lot. They told her that they would hold him up to the window so that we could see him and he could see us. We were told that we were going to see Michael, not to say good-bye to him. Enroute to the hospital, I was still trying to get over the shock of learning that he was still alive! When we got to the hospital parking lot, we all scrambled out of Aunt Meg's car and stood where we could get a clear view of the window where our brother would soon appear.

Suddenly, Michael was there, being held up on both sides by two people dressed in white. Even at a distance, I could see his eyes widen in amazement! We waved frantically and called to him as if he could really hear us! We were overjoyed! Later, we learned that just seeing us and learning that we were still alive had given Michael a new will to live! To everyone's amazement, he embarked upon the road to a remarkable recovery! Michael had believed that Ronnie and I had been killed the same night we lost our mother. No one had even mentioned us when they came to visit him in the Intensive Care ward. No one had told him that Tony didn't kill everybody! Because he thought that we were all dead, he thought he had no reason to live either! But, he did! He had us! He just didn't know it! When he found out, Michael was determined to recover!

"There he is!" Wayne squealed, waving excitedly.

I waved and grinned from ear to ear.

Ronnie, as usual, clung to Aunt Meg's skirt and jumped up and down. I looked down at him and wondered if he even knew who Michael was. He seemed to have forgotten Mama. But right then, it wasn't important whether or not he knew who Michael was. I was too happy to see my brother! I yelled out his name and jumped and down, too!

Aunt Meg, who seemed to cry easily those days, became very emotional. Her eyes filled with tears as she looked up from Michael's frail figure in the window, back to the three exhilarated children around her. All too soon, the people at the window removed Michael from our view and put him back into the bed. We were disappointed, but thrilled at having seen our brother... still alive!

A few days later, I wrote my first song. It was entitled, "What Now?" I can still remember some of the words and most of the melody. It went something like, "In a world of confusion, a word of illusion, what now?" I'm not sure I really knew what the words meant, but I believe that God put them in my heart and I wrote them in a song to a melody I heard in my head. I played the song for Mr. Mathis and he was speechless! He couldn't believe that I had just made it up! He asked me if I knew what the words meant.

I told him I wasn't sure, but I knew exactly what I was trying to say!

When Michael came home, our lives began to take on some sense of normalcy. We adjusted to being with Aunt Meg and Uncle Harrison all of the time. The adjustment was probably most difficult for them! After all, they had had no children and suddenly, they had four! For a while, things seemed to be progressing smoothly. I had found a new love… music! Wayne and Michael spent endless days playing ball, and Ronnie had Aunt Meg, b.k.a. Mama. We still missed our mother, but we had accepted the fact that she wasn't coming back. It wasn't as if we had any other choice.

I have really wrestled with some of the things I felt I needed to write about. I hesitated to open the door any wider because some of the monsters still lurking behind it have caused me just as much pain as that caused me by my father. Perhaps I was not sure whether or not I wanted to reveal those things because I knew that any healing gained by me would possibly bring grief to others. I gave it considerable thought, and I realized that there was no way to "partially" clean out the closet, removing only those things I chose to remove. If I cleaned house at all, I had to clean house completely! Otherwise, the job was only half-done. What would have been the point?

Some time in March, about a month after I began peeling away the layers of my past, I decided to discuss a particular experience with my very close friend, Ophelia. As I said, I had wrestled with the notion of writing about some other things.

Ophelia and I were together at her office late one Sunday evening. I mentioned something to her that I thought I had told her about some time ago. We have been friends for sixteen years. I assumed that if anyone knew all there was to know about me, it was she! Boy, was I wrong! She literally fell onto a sofa in her office, as if the wind had been knocked out of her when I mentioned to her that I had been molested as a child.

We had been talking about my writing about all of the "stuff" which had somehow surfaced as a result of my meeting Debra. Ophelia encouraged me to write, to get it all out, and in the process, heal the numerous wounds in my life. She had been well acquainted with the incident in which Mama and Grandmama died. We had talked about that years ago. I took for granted that she knew that and more. But how could she have known everything? There was so much I had suppressed or conveniently forgotten about. I told Ophelia that I had been struggling with the idea of including my experience of being molested in my writing. I told her that I wasn't sure if I should because I felt that too many people would be hurt to find out about it.

"What!?" she shrieked, sinking down onto the couch. "What? Molested?" Her look of disbelief convinced me that I had never mentioned that to her.

"I thought I told you," I said, exhaling deeply. I sat down on the sofa beside her. "I really thought I had told you about that."

"No," Ophelia said, "you never told me anything about that!" She got up. "Don't tell me anymore! I can't take it!" Agitatedly, she moved around the office, collecting her things so that we could leave.

"I don't know what to do," I said, following her into the front of the office building. "There is just so much inside of me... so much I can hardly stand it." The mushroom was still there.

"Who?" she said, spinning around to face me. "Who was it?" Then, just as suddenly as she had asked, she raised her right hand, as if taking an oath, "Never mind, don't tell me! I don't want to know! If I don't know, I won't have to think about it!"

I knew she didn't want to know. But I wanted to tell her. I needed her to know, but I didn't have to tell her after all. She told me.

"Not Uncle Harrison?"

I looked at her. It was him, but he had not been the only one. For a moment, my mind went back to a cousin who had fondled me in his backyard when I was nine or ten years old. After Mama died, we had to spend our summer days at Aunt Betty's house while Aunt Meg and Uncle Harrison went to work. Her oldest son would often "trap" me in the house while the other kids played outside. He would back me into a corner and touch me in places I knew he should not, telling me that it would make me feel better! I was supposed to be so depressed about the loss of my mother, and I guess he just wanted to do his part in helping me to get over it! I always struggled to resist his advances, but being bigger and stronger, he knew how to hold me while he touched me in secret places. I hated him! Until now, I have never told anyone about it. In fact, I purposely tried to forget about it. I tried to forget about him, too! I decided that he was just a pervert and consoled myself with the fact that every family probably had one just like him! After that, I did my best to avoid being alone with him. That became easier when he graduated from high school and enlisted in the U.S. Army. I was relieved when word came that he had been shipped overseas! Whenever he came back home for a visit, I always found something else to do so that I wouldn't have to accompany Aunt Meg over to his mother's house to see him.

It has been many, many years since I have seen him. Not long ago, I went to his mother's funeral. He didn't even bother to show up! Before she died, she told me that he had become very distant from her and his brothers, as well. She believed that he was dealing with some "demons" in his life and could not stand to be in the presence of the "God" within her. I was tempted to tell her that the demons were probably not a recent development. He had had them for a long, long time!

"Lord, Jesus!" Ophelia cried, snatching up her purse from a nearby chair. "Let's get out of here!"

In the car, I told her again that I thought she had already known. I don't know why I said that. It was evident that she hadn't. But there was something she did know. She had spent a lot of time with Aunt Meg and she knew that there was something not-quite-right between the two of us. Ophelia had never known what it was. She had heard Aunt Meg say things which suggested some animosity towards me. Although Aunt Meg had never elaborated, Ophelia knew that there was something there. Now, she knew what that something was.

"Lord!" she exclaimed, gripping the steering wheel. "Please tell me there was no penetration!"

"No," I answered. "It never came to that. Mostly, he just touched me while he masturbated. He never had intercourse with me." Even so, it had still gone too far, I thought.

"Well, thank God for that!" she said.

"Yeah," I sighed, suddenly feeling very tired.

"I knew she wasn't happy," Ophelia said, "but I just didn't know why."

"She thought I was trying to cause problems between them," I explained. "I don't know... I know she couldn't have thought I wanted him!"

"No, I know she didn't think that!"

"She didn't believe me when I told her, you know," I said, looking out of the window.

"Yes, she did," Ophelia interjected. "She believed you. That's why she acted so hateful towards you."

"Because she knew it was true?"

"Yeah."

I didn't say anything for a moment. I looked out of the window at the moonlit sky. God, I wondered, where were you when all of that was happening to me? "It wasn't my fault," I said, shaking my head. "She acted like it was my fault and it wasn't!"

"When did this happen?"

"I don't know exactly when it started, but I was fifteen when it stopped." I didn't tell her any of the morbid details. I didn't want the filthy words to come out of my mouth! I didn't

69

tell her that for a long time, I hated the man who had taken me and my brothers in to care for us after we became orphans. I didn't tell her that I looked at him with disgust, even when he was looking directly at me! When I talked to him, I was blatantly disrespectful. From my tone of voice, when I spoke to him, I may as well have been cursing! He knew that I hated him, too. He saw it in my eyes. He heard it in my voice. Aunt Meg acted as if she thought I was just being a disrespectful juvenile, but in her heart, she had to have known better! Instead of hearing me out, however, she chose to believe that I was making it all up, to get attention! Uncle Harrison concurred with her. After all, they reasoned, I had been through so much trauma already, my "wild imaginings" and accusations were probably due to mental and emotional instability, which most likely resulted from the tragic experience.

When I was fifteen, Uncle Harrison taught me to drive. One day, after I had long tired of telling Aunt Meg that her husband was sneaking into the room I shared with my brothers to "bother" me, I decided to take matters into my own hands. She had called me a whore, a lying whore and a slut! To my face, she had called me every nasty, hateful name she could think of! Again, my world was crashing down around me! I was sick and tired of his touching me! I had gotten to the point where I didn't even want him to look at me!

I was sitting behind the wheel of our white '68 Impala, my foot on the brake. He was sitting across from me on the passenger side. Looking straight ahead at the red dirt road in front of us, I said, "I'm tired of you messing with me." My voice was unusually calm and steady. I could tell that he was trying to act as if he didn't know what I was talking about. But, he knew. I went on. "I'm tired of telling Aunt Meg and her not doing anything about it. I want you to stop. I don't ever want you to touch me again!"

He shifted nervously in the seat, but still said nothing.

I waited for a response.

Still, he said nothing.

I turned to look at him. "If you ever touch me again, I'm going to kill you," I said. "I mean it, too! I'm going to kill you and then, I'm going to kill myself, because I would rather be dead than for you to touch me again!" I said the words and I believe he knew that I meant them.

He never said a word. He never touched me again.

Throughout the years, it has difficult for me to think about that. I understand why a lot of people who have been molested find it so hard to talk about. It hurts! It hurts because the person who has chosen to violate you is usually someone you thought you could trust! This is particularly hard for me because the violator is still very much a part of my life. If someone had looked into my future and told me that I would end up taking care of "Harry" some day, I would have never believed them! If they had predicted that some queer twist of fate would bring us together under the circumstances which it finally did, I would have called them a liar! It has taken a great deal of strength, more than I thought I had, to forgive him for what he did to me as a child. In my heart, I believe I have been able to forgive him. God knows, I have tried to. Unfortunately, it has not been as easy to forget.

The first time I saw "The Color Purple," I cried all the way through it! I cried when good things happened and I cried when bad things happened to the sisters, Celie and Nettie. I can remember feeling sorry for Celie as she was sexually abused by the man she believed to be her father. I knew, too well, how the character must have felt. I, like Celie, had accepted it as something that had been my fate to endure. I could also relate to the character Sophia that had been so convincingly portrayed by Oprah Winfrey. I have watched that movie at least twenty times and I cringed each time Sophia told Miss Celie about her having had to fight off the sexual advances of her uncles and cousins. Big, bold Sophia! She had suffered so much abuse in her life, she was willing to kill her husband, Harpo, dead, before she let him beat her! My heart went out to her! I empathized with her! I used to **be** Sophia.

71

Even after Harry got the message, things did not get much better between Aunt Meg and me. I ran away from home several times, only to be found running through the streets of Columbus in the middle of the night! Once, she told me to go, to get out! So, I went! I just started walking. It was almost midnight. About an hour later, halfway across town, Uncle Harrison drove up on me, Michael on the passenger side. He saw me duck into the darkness on the side of a house. He rolled the window down and called to me.

"Nesi!" his shrill voice rang into the darkness. "Nesi, we can see you over there! Come on and go back home!"

Reluctantly, I came out of hiding and crawled into the back seat. When we got home, Aunt Meg was waiting with tears in her eyes, as if she was actually upset that I had tried to run away! I didn't believe her! She was the one who had told me to get out in the first place! What had she expected me to do? What did she want from me? I couldn't figure her out! Needless to say, by that time, I had come to the conclusion that adults were the most confused bunch of people God had ever created! I prayed that I wouldn't act so stupid when I became an adult. I always try to remember that prayer when my thirteen year old son drives me to the brink of hysteria!

That night, I went to bed, still wearing my clothes. Every time I turned over in the top bunk, I could hear Michael stir in the bunk beneath me. I think he was trying to keep an eye on me to make sure I didn't get up and try to leave again. I felt a little better knowing that he wanted me to say. It reminded me of my promise to take care of Ronnie. If I intended to follow through on it, I would have to stick around.

I can remember numerous attempts I made to attain Aunt Meg's love and acceptance. I went out of my way to do things around the house in search of her approval. It became an obsession for me! Without being told, I would clean up behind my brothers. While they played outside, I was in the house ironing! When she came home, she would criticize the ironing I had done, arguing that I had done it wrong! No room was ever clean enough! No cornbread was ever baked done enough! No towels were ever folded tightly enough! Nothing was ever enough! But Lord knows, I tried! There's an old spiritual which says, "If I never reach perfection, Lord, I tried! The writer had to have had me in mind when he penned those words! I bent over backwards and performed cartwheels for Aunt Meg, yet it profited me nothing!

I listened as she discussed me with her friends on the telephone. Knowing nothing better, I was sure they all believed that I was the "sorry, good-for-nothing" she made me out to be! My heart ached every time she told me to my face that I was "just like" my father! I believed she hated me because I knew she hated him! I cried myself to sleep so many nights in that top bunk bed. I couldn't tell anyone, but Jesus, what I was going through, because there was no one on earth for me to tell! My brothers, I thought, were just children! They couldn't possibly understand. Somewhere, somehow, I had grown up and beyond them — oh, not chronologically, but certainly emotionally. I had no choice! I grew up because my world had grown up around me. I could not afford to be a child any longer. I had no one to take care of me, but myself.

Beginning at age twelve, I spent my Summers working. During that first Summer, I worked for my fifth grade teacher, Mrs. Fluellen. I was a sort of "Florence Nightingale" for her mother, *Miss Jenny,* a fragile, elderly white woman who had fallen and broken her hip. I slept on a small twin bed in one corner of the room with the kind, petite woman, who called me "Darlene," for some obscure reason. When she called to me in the night, I groggily crawled out of the bed and got the bed pan for her. Once, I was so sleepy, I put the cold, chrome pan backwards under her tiny, pink and very wrinkled bottom! In her gentle, soft-spoken way, she said, "Darlene, that's not right, honey!" That woke me up! I realized my error and tried to correct it as quickly as I could, but it was too late! She peed all over her bed and my hands too! It's funny now, but it wasn't funny to me then! There is nothing amusing about having some little old lady pee on your hands!

Every Summer, throughout my senior year in high school, I got a job through a government funded city youth opportunity program. At the close of each school year, I looked forward to getting a job. Since I could type pretty fast and accurately, I began to get office jobs each summer. I learned to save my money from those assignments. At the end of the summer, I would ask Aunt Meg to take me shopping for school clothes. After she had cursed to her satisfaction, she would usually give in and take me. It felt good to know I was buying my own clothes with my own money. I felt very independent! I guess that was what she meant when she later told me that I had always acted like I never needed anyone. In a way, I suppose I owe a lot of that to her. It doesn't make much sense to need someone when you already know that they won't be there for you. I wish I had told her that when I had the chance.

"And ye shall know the truth, and the truth shall make you free." John 8:32

Four

After I informed Mr. Wimbush that because of his story, I had found a sister I had never known about, he was excited about doing a follow-up story. He insisted upon talking to Debra and her mother. The result of the conversations with them and me was another story. He asked us to come down to the newspaper so that we could be photographed for the article.

Early that morning, I had asked Darrell to accompany me to the newspaper office to meet Debra so that we could have our picture taken together.

"Why?" he asked. He was anxious to get over to his brother, Jerry's house so that he could work on his '68 Mustang. Darrell loves that car! We joke that it is his "other woman!" I knew that he would much rather go over and spend time with "her," than to go down to the newspaper with me, but I needed him.

"I just need you to go with me," I said, sitting down on the sofa beside him in our living room. "To tell the truth, I'm a little nervous," I confessed.

"Nervous? About what?" Darrell asked. "It's not like it's going to be your first time meeting Debra." He picked up a magazine from the coffee table and began thumbing through it.

"I know," I said, "but I'm still a little jittery about this whole thing." I was not "jittery," I was mortified! I couldn't explain to my husband about the "mushroom" blossoming inside me. I didn't know how to. I just needed to know that he would be there, beside me, when I saw my sister again and felt my father's presence again. I already knew he would be there, waiting for me.

Darrell didn't understand my apprehension, but conceded nonetheless. "Okay," he said, "I'll go. But I still don't know what you're so afraid of."

I didn't tell him about the anxieties I had been experiencing ever since I had met Debra. I didn't tell him about the door that she had unlocked. I still haven't really told him. I've asked him to read some of what I've been writing, but he doesn't want to. I explained to him that I felt it would help him to understand how, and possibly, why I feel the way I do. He flatly refused to read it. He said he didn't need to understand me in order to love me. I need him to love me, too, of course, but I believe he needs to understand me in order to do that. I'm sure of it! He did say, however, that if this writing eventually becomes a book, he will read it. I've been praying for the Lord to make that a reality, for more reasons than one.

When Mr. Wimbush walked into the waiting area and saw Debra and I sitting together on the sofa, he smiled, "Yes, yes, I see the resemblance!"

Debra laughed and I smiled, somewhat uneasily.

He ushered Debra, Darrell and me into the same room where Darrell and I had been photographed for the first article, the story that had brought Debra and I together in the first place. The photographer came in and instructed us to sit close together, on a pair of stools which had been placed in front of the camera. She put her arm around my shoulder as we both held and pretended to look at a copy of the original newspaper article. The photographer told us to smile and smile, we did. Debra was a little more enthusiastic than I. After seeing the published photograph, I admitted that her smile seemed to radiate genuine happiness over having found the sister she thought she would never know. My smile was a little strained, to say the least. It wasn't that I was not excited about having her in my life. On the contrary, I was. It was the rest of the stuff that came along with her - the past and its demons!

After the photo shoot, we left the building together. Darrell decided to walk down the street to a barber shop so that he could get a haircut. I drove Debra to a nearby restaurant where she was supposed to meet her daughter shortly thereafter.

As we sat across from each other in the quaint little restaurant, we talked about the irony of us finding each other and about how miraculous everything seemed to be. I told her where

I had been in my life and she briefed me about her own. Of course, there were thirty-eight years to cover, and we both knew that we would never be able to catch each other up in a single conversation over a cup of coffee! However, since she had to wait for her daughter and I had to wait on Darrell's barber, we decided to get started.

There was so much to learn about this young woman who smiled my smile back at me! She told me that she had never been married, but she had had four children, two girls and two boys. She had had another child, a little girl who had died when she was just a baby.

I told Debra that I was in my second marriage and that I had two, well no, actually three, sons. I joked that I had inherited Little Darrell when I married his dad.

We both had attended local high schools, which, as it turned out, had been rivals on both the football field and basketball courts! I remarked that, at some point in time, we had probably been at some of the same athletic events, at the same time, without even knowing it! As we talked, I discovered that my sister and I had lived incredibly different lives! We had been as far as the east is from the west in our own individual existences, yet God had brought us together in a climatic result through a series of unfortunately events!

I related to Debra a telephone conversation I had had with the reporter, Mr. Wimbush. I had been telling him that God had really done some awesome things in my life and it was very difficult not to tell people about it. I just ouldn't keep it to myself! Mr. Wimbush, too, had a testimony h he readily shared with me. He had lost his teenage daughter the previous year in a most unexpected manner. She was a high school student who was attending the Alabama Shakespeare Festival on a field trip. Without warning, she suffered a fatal heart attack! Mr. Wimbush, his wife and their family were devastated! In the midst of their heartbreak, he told me that he realized that God had a way of taking bad situations and making good out of them. He said that had happened with his daughter and her untimely death. Even though her life was short-lived, she had been an angel in his life! During the short time she had been entrusted to him and his wife, she had been a blessing to them -- a blessing which they can still appreciate today! Because of his daughter, his faith had been increased!

Mr. Wimbush reminded me of the Bible story in which Joseph was sold into slavery by his jealous brothers, only to have God's love and mercy preserve him. In the end, Joseph's brothers had to seek his help in order that they might survive the terrible famine which threatened to destroy the inhabitants of the land. He said that although the devil meant Joseph's experience for bad, God meant it for good! Just hearing him say that gave a boost to my own faith!

As he spoke, I thought about how Satan, through Tony, and others in my past, had tried to destroy my life. I realized that on numerous occasions, he had been in my presence, trying to destroy and belittle the blessings that God kept right on sending my way. I also recognized that despite my experiences, despite the tragedies, despite the grief, my faith had wavered, but never dissipated! I still trusted God with my life! Now, I trust Him even more!

I told Debra that I believe God allowed us to find each other at a time He knew we would be ready for such a tremendous revelation! I believe that because finding her forced me to deal with many emotions and experiences in my own life which, had they surfaced before, would have probably destroyed me completely! Before now, I don't think I would have been able to weather the storm. God knew the time had come and He knew that both Debra and I were ready, even if we didn't know it. All the time, He had been preparing us for a destiny that had been coming since the beginning of creation.

In our conversation that day, Debra mentioned that she was seeing someone whom she believed would some day become her husband. I didn't want to burst her bubble or anything, but I commented that although I didn't know him, she should pray and ask God if this man is indeed her husband before she takes a major step like marriage! I went on to tell her the story of how I met Darrell.

After having lived in Los Angeles, California for a little over five years, I returned to Columbus, Georgia. Aunt Meg had a heart attack in November of 1990. In December, she passed away. After talking with Harry, I decided to stay in Columbus. In 1991, I decided to go back to college. When I finally decided that teaching was to be my career choice, I pursued it with a newfound passion!

A young man, whom I had been romantically involved with while residing in Los Angeles, decided that he simply could not live without me, so he followed me to Georgia. He showed up quite unexpectedly. We had not dated in several months prior to my leaving California. But, he came to Georgia with a ring and promises of love and marriage. It was not very long before I realized that he was not the one for me because we actually had very little in common. He didn't know the Lord and quite frankly, he had no desire to make His acquaintance! He was only minimally interested in my son, Tjai. Minimally was just not enough!

After some real soul searching, I prayed and asked God to take control of my life. I promised Him aloud that I would do His will and I asked that He let it prevail! I confessed that I did not want a boyfriend, and admitted that I no longer wanted to date anyone. I was convinced that my seven year old son needed a father and I needed a "helpmate," a husband. So, I asked God to send me my husband! As incredible as it may seem, that's exactly what I did! After doing so, I waited for God to answer my prayer.

It is true that you should be careful what you ask for! I say that because no sooner than I had asked God to take control of my life, I realized He did just that! Like a tempest, He began to move. "Mr. California" had just arrived, and he was leaving just as quickly! God removed the desire I had for him from my heart. I knew that he was not what I wanted and there was no future in our relationship! I realized that it had been purely "physical," the worst kind of addiction a woman could have! After he left, I felt so relieved! I was ready to go on with my life, so I got busy!

Primarily, there were four things that I focused upon. I worked hard at being a good mother to my son and a good student in college. I tried to take care of my dad, as I had promised my mom that I would. Lastly, but certainly not least, I worked at being a faithful servant to God. I committed myself to skillfully dividing my time between being Director of Music at my church, as well as Director of Youth Ministries. I didn't have time to worry about having or missing a man in my life. I believed that God would set things right when He decided to do so.

One Friday, Tjai, my dad, and I went out to dinner. We had plans to go to a movie afterward. We went to a Shoney's Restaurant near our house. I remember walking into the restaurant and noticing a rather large group of people sitting together on one side. As we passed by them, I glanced over at the people, who were busy talking among themselves. I couldn't help but notice that they seemed to be very attentive to us, but at that time, I really thought nothing much of it. After our waitress had seated us and had taken our order, I noticed that one of the young men in the large dinner party was looking over in our direction. Tjai and I were sitting across from my dad, so we could see him clearly. Tjai, too, noticed that the young man was staring at us. He nudged me in the side and whispered, "Mom, look at that man over there, looking at you!"

"Don't stare!" I warned him, toying with the napkin I had put over my lap.

He was persistent though. "But that man over there is staring at you! Look!"

I looked up and met his dark eyes. Not only was he staring, but other members of his group had joined him and were now looking in our direction, too. I felt my cheeks becoming flushed! I looked back down at the white linen napkin, trying to compose myself.

I had decided to eat from the salad bar. Tjai wanted some rice pilaf from the adjoining hot food bar, so we both got up to fix our plates. I had just reached for a salad plate when I felt my son's sharp elbow in my side.

"Look!" he whispered, excitedly. "Here he comes!"

To my surprise, the stranger was walking towards us at the salad bar.

"Excuse me," he said, with an accent I was not quite sure of. "I hope I'm not making you uncomfortable or anything, but I just wanted to come over here and tell you that you are a very beautiful woman."

Not only was he making me uncomfortable, but I was convinced that he was giving me a very old line! I wasn't having any of it! "Yes, you are making me uncomfortable!" I almost snapped at him.

"Well," he went on, ignoring my sarcasm, "I don't mean to, but I wanted to come over and talk to you for a minute. I thought that maybe I could get your phone number. Maybe we could go out to dinner or something?"

I tried to avoid his gaze. My hands trembled as I attempted to put a tongfull of crisp green lettuce on my plate. Dinner? Was he kidding? I didn't know him and I was having a hard time just fixing a salad in front of him. Was he smiling? I wasn't sure. I refused to look directly at him to see.

Tjai was giggling.

"I was trying to have dinner right now," I said, as calmly as I could. For some strange reason, my heart was palpitating!

"Well, why don't you just give me your number and--"

"I don't have a pen," I said, interrupting him.

He hesitated for a couple of seconds. "What's your name?" he asked. From the tone of his voice, I could tell that he **was** smiling.

"Denise," I said. "This is my son, Tjai," I added, gesturing towards my seven year old.

"Well, Denise," he began, as if he knew something about me, "when you walked in, I noticed that you had a purse. You might have a pen in there." He winked at Tjai.

Tjai smiled back at him.

I still didn't look up at him, but I could tell he was amused. I heard it in his voice. I realized that he was not going to give up very easily. "All right," I said. I turned and walked back to the table where my dad had begun eating. I didn't realize that I still had not made a salad until I sat the cold salad plate down on the table. My dad looked up at us and smiled. "This is my dad," I said to the stranger. "And your name is?"

"Darrell," he said, offering his hand to my father. "'Nice to meet you, sir," he said.

Harry took his hand and shook it.

A little startled at his manners, I glanced at him sideways, but not too closely. After all, I didn't want him to think I was too interested! I picked up my purse and dug through it in search of a pen.

Tjai sat down at the table, a broad smile on his face. He didn't seem to mind the interruption of our dinner the slightest bit!

When I found a pen, I scrawled my phone number on one of the white paper napkins our waitress had left on the table and handed it to him.

"Thank you," Darrell said. He smiled at me. "I'll call you soon."

For a brief moment, my eyes met his, but I quickly looked away. The people at his table were watching. I glanced over at them and someone actually waved at me! I sat down, red-faced! I could not even watch him walk away. I felt so embarrassed, I ate very little of my dinner that evening.

Three weeks passed and I had not heard from Darrell. I had practically given up on him. I decided that he had probably been just a "flake" or something! I had gone to work at my part-time job the Monday after our initial acquaintance and related the episode to some of my co-workers. For the next several days, they asked if I had heard from my "mystery man." I told them that I hadn't. After a couple of weeks had passed, they, too, presumed that he was a "flake" and stopped asking. I said nothing else about him. On Friday, exactly three weeks after we met, Darrell called me at work.

"You probably don't remember me," said the voice on the other end of the phone, "but I met you a few weeks ago at Shoneys." The accent was definitely southern.

"Oh I remember you," I said, positioning the receiver on my shoulder so that I could continue typing away on the computer keyboard. "What I don't remember is giving you this phone number," I said. I distinctly remembered giving him my home phone number.

"Yes, I know," he responded, lightheartedly. "But, I called your house and your dad gave me this number. He said I could reach you there... He was right!" He was smiling again, I could tell.

"Oh," I said, wondering what my dad was doing at home. He was supposed to be on the shop floor working. He was head designer at the florist where we both worked. I didn't even know he had left the shop and gone home.

Darrell invited me to go to lunch with him. I declined, giving him some lame excuse. I said something about having had a big breakfast and not really being hungry. The real reason I didn't want to go with him was my appearance. That morning, I had pulled my medium length brown hair back into a ponytail. I was wearing jeans and a tee-shirt, definitely "underdressed" for a lunch date! I wasn't even wearing makeup! I didn't remember what he looked like, but if I was going to lunch with him, I preferred to look a little more presentable myself!

"Maybe another time," I suggested.

"Nope," he said, firmly, "I'm taking you to lunch today."

Before I could respond, he continued.

"Your dad told me where you are. Now, if you don't go to lunch with me, I'll have to just come over there anyway." His voice was "matter-of-fact," but I could tell he was dead serious!

What? I thought. Just who does he think he is? I asked myself. I was speechless! No one had ever done that to me before, and I must admit, I was a little intrigued by his boldness. I agreed to meet him at a restaurant in the nearby mall. I hung up the phone, a little embarrassed by my anxiousness to get there to see him. On the way, I tried to summon his face into my mind, but for the life of me, I couldn't! I parked my Chevy Cavalier in the mall parking lot and walked a short distance to the entrance nearest the restaurant where we had agreed to meet.

I pushed through the heavy glass doors and went inside the festive-looking mall. I walked over to one side and stood there, looking around. Through my dark glasses, I had a pretty good view of the lunchtime traffic. Several people were standing in front of the restaurant doors. Suddenly, I noticed a young, casually dressed man, walking towards me. Surely, that can't be him, I thought. He was gorgeous! As he got closer to me, a smile crossed his face.

"Denise?"

"Yes," I said, as my heart decided to pound in my throat.

"How are you doing?" he asked, taking my hand in his.

I felt lightheaded. "Oh, fine," I lied, trying to sound as gracious as I possibly could. "And you?"

"Better now," he said, pulling me close to him. He hugged me.

I inhaled him. The aroma was enticing!

Darrell had a wide and beautiful smile! He was very handsome and equally as charming! We sat across from each other at the restaurant and I was amazed at how relaxed we seemed to be with each other. He asked me about myself and Tjai. I told him that we had been in Columbus, my native home, for less than a year. I told that I had decided to stay in Georgia to care for my dad after my mom died. I didn't want to say "too much," but I did tell him that Tjai's father and I were divorced.

Darrell told me a little about himself. At the time, he was stationed at Fort Benning, a nearby military installation. Originally from Mississippi, he had been in Georgia for a few months. He also had a young son. He, too was divorced. I enjoyed listening to him talk about himself and his family in his comical way. He was very funny and we laughed a lot, a little too loudly at times! He enthralled me with details of his visits abroad on a recent European tour with the United States Army. I envied his walks along the streets of Paris and weekend excursions to the Netherlands! What I wouldn't have given to have visited Europe! The way Darrell talked about it made me wistful.

We both noticed that our waitress was overly attentive. She had already been to our table twice since our food had arrived. Darrell joked that if she came back anytime soon, he was going to invite her to join us for lunch! I laughed. I had just put a forkful of salad in my mouth, trying to be as demure as I could, like any woman who wanted to make a good first impression, when Darrell asked me if I wanted to know how old he was.

I thought the question was a strange one. "Why?" I asked. "Do you want to tell me?" I picked up another forkful of salad. It was delicious! Either the greens were the most succulent I had ever tasted or I was starved!

He smiled. "I just thought you might want to know."

"Why?" I asked. "You must want to know how old I am," I reasoned, still chewing.

"I suspect you're about thirty," he said.

Thirty...that was a pretty good guess. I was thirty-four. I told him so, between bites.

"Well," he said, "I'm twenty four."

At once, I began to choke on my food!

Darrell picked up my water glass and handed it to me. "Is that because of your salad or because of what I just said?"

I took the glass from him. "Both!" I said, quickly taking a gulp. Twenty four! Immediately, I knew that it was not very likely that anything would develop between us. I had never even considered dating anyone that much younger than me. I stared at him.

He searched my face for a clue into my thoughts. "Well?"

"Well, what?" I cleared my throat.

"So what do you think" he asked.

I didn't know what I thought. I shrugged. "I don't think anything."

He looked amused. "You're surprised," he said.

Shocked was a more appropriate word. "Oh, no," I lied. I would have guessed you were somewhere around that," I laughed, uncomfortably, hoping he couldn't see the drops of perspiration forming on my forehead.

"Have you ever dated anyone younger than you?" Darrell asked, taking a sip of his water.

"No," I answered, "not really." I lifted my glass to my lips and drank. My eyes lowered as I pretended to be interested in something in the bottom of my glass.

He was smiling now. "Well, you know that they say!"

I had no idea who "they" were or what "they" said. "No, what?"

"First time for everything!" He grinned across the table at me.

I smiled back, but I knew that nothing could possibly come of it. He was a nice guy, but he couldn't be the one, I thought. Twenty-four? Humph!

After lunch, Darrell walked me to my car in the crowded parking lot. I thanked him for lunch and told him that I had truly enjoyed it. I really had! In fact, I had had a wonderful time! It was too bad it couldn't go any further, I thought. He was not only very good-looking and extremely charming, he was funny, too! As he kissed me on the cheek, I inhaled him, again. He said that he would call me later. This time, I watched him walk away. I went back to work with my head in the clouds!

To my utter disbelief, Darrell and I soon became an "item." It just happened! We felt so right together, the ten-year difference in our ages didn't seem to matter. In many ways, he was much older than me! He loved listening to the Blues, something I had never gotten into before. He loved sitting and talking to elderly people. He and Harry always seemed to find something to talk about! I wondered what they had in common.

Darrell and I certainly had a lot in common! Besides both coming from "marriages from hell" and both having sons, neither of us particularly cared for the "nightclub" scene. We enjoyed doing a lot of the same things. He wanted someone he could grow with and accumulate something with. So did I! We both enjoyed walks in the rain and watching movies. Darrell was kind, thoughtful, and considerate. Most importantly, he fell in love with Tjai and Tjai fell in love with him!

"But seek ye first the kingdom of God, and His righteousness; and all these things shall be added unto you. Matt. 6:33

On December 22, 1991, I knew that Darrell was my husband. It was early one Sunday morning, around seven o'clock. I had gotten up at the crack of dawn to finish up some wings for some of the little girls who were going to be angels in the

Christmas play at church, later that evening. I was kneeling on the floor, sprinkling glitter over lines of white glue on a pair of wings when I had the distinct feeling that I was being watched. I looked around at the diamond-shaped window on the front door and saw Darrell watching me. I had no idea how long he had been standing there. I got up off my knees and went to open the door.

"What are you doing here? I asked, hugging him. We had been seeing each other for the past five months, almost every day.

"I came to see Tjai," he said, holding me close to him for a moment.

I felt so good in his arms. I held onto him and to the moment.

Tjai was still asleep. "It's just seven o'clock," I said. "He hasn't gotten up yet."

All too son, he released me and stepped aside so that I could close the door. Darrell was holding a small, brown, paper bag in one hand. "I need to see him," he said. "Would you wake him up for me?"

"Okay," I said, wondering what was going on. I left him in the living room and went into Tjai's room to wake him up.

On the previous night, Darrell had brought Tjai and I home from a trip to nearby Atlanta. After we had pulled into the drive-way and gotten out of the car, Tjai had tossed a rock in Darrell's direction, nearly hitting him in the head! When I walked back into the living room with my son behind me, I was astonished to see Darrell reach into the brown paper bag and pull out a sling shot! I thought, either he must have forgotten that Tjai had almost hit him in the head last night, or perhaps Tjai hadn't missed after all! A sling shot?

"Hey, Tjai," Darrell said, sitting down on the sofa. "Come here. I brought you something." He held his gift out to Tjai.

Still groggy, Tjai took the sling shot into his hands and sat down on the sofa next to Darell. His eyes widened as he realized what the object was.

I moved away from them to stand near the piano. I leaned against it and watched the two of them.

"Now, Tjai," Darrell began, "I got this for you because I want to teach you something about responsibility."

Tjai's eyes roved from the new sling shot in his hands to Darrell's face and back.

Darrell took it from him. It was still attached to a brightly-colored card with two twister ties. He turned it over and began to read the instructions on the back out loud.

Tjai listened, intently, blinking the sleep away from his eyes. He looked at the back of the card, along with Darrell

As I watched them, I felt tears fill my eyes. At that moment, I knew that Darrell was truly my husband... the one I had asked God for. I knew it! It was as if God Himself was speaking to me, affirming the cognition of my heart! As Darrell sat and explained to my son how important it was to be responsible, the Spirit was saying to me, "That is your husband!" I can't explain what the voice of God sounds like, but I felt Him speak to me. Despite my initial disbelief, I knew that something had come of our meeting each other. I knew that Darrell was the one! God had sent him to me! As I stood next to the piano, in our living-groom, and watched and listened to the man who would eventually become my husband, joy filled my heart. Somehow, I didn't really think I deserved to feel what I was feeling at that moment, but I made up my mind to relish it while it lasted!

I have told this story several times before, particularly to young women who complain that they are still looking for "Mr. Right." I have shared my testimony with them, in hopes that they will be convinced that they, too, must ask God to send them their mate, instead of trying to find one on their own. I admonish them to let God do the job that only He is wise enough to know how to do! I am quick to tell them that I can't introduce them to anyone because I don't know what tomorrow will bring, but God does! He knows what lies ahead and what that man or woman will do in the future! I recently told a friend of mine that God is the best judge of character because we don't know what people are really capable of doing. That is why we must learn to trust Him to send us the person He has already chosen for us! When we try to handle that ourselves, we usually make a mess of things! Both Darrell and I did that before we met each other. We ended up with two other people who were really wrong for us and the result was disastrous! I know! My "Mr. Right" was as wrong as two left shoes in two totally different sizes! It was not until I asked God to be the keeper of and to watch over the affairs of my heart that I really got it right! He sent me a real "soul mate!" He sent me Darrell!

God has really blessed our relationship. Although we know that we are "soul mates," like any other couple, we have had our differences. We are still individuals with distinctly different personalities. As Pastor Thompson told us in our prenuptial counseling session, marriage is the coming together of two people who have chosen to become one. Anyone can tell you that any time two people try to share the same space, there are bound to be conflicts and differences of opinion. Just the act of sharing can sometimes cause problems!

We have recently learned how to share each other's space, as well as give each other room to be individuals. It was a long and sometimes tedious process of learning on both of our parts. We had to learn something about each other's individual past. I had to learn that Darrell's background is very different from mine. He grew up in a home where his male role model was his high school coach. He worshipped the ground that Coach Levander German walked on! He still does today! In fact, in tribute to him, we had to name our youngest son, Christopher, after him! Darrell brought his past experiences under Coach German's leadership into our relationship.

I brought my own experiences, regardless of how awful some of them are, with me. I thank God that He gave me a husband like Darrell. He knew that I was going to need someone just like him in my life. It is because of the kind of man that my husband is that I have the space and the courage necessary to face my past and its demons. God waited until I had a secure marriage and a family to love and support me during a time when He knew I would need it most!

Five

I talked to my oldest brother, Wayne, one day and told him that I had decided to write about the incredible things that have happened to me. He was excited about that. He agreed with me that I do have a story to tell. I assured him that he could look forward to seeing some of the crazy antics of our childhood in print some day.

"Oh yeah? Like what?" he asked.

"Like the time you poured that pot of hot scalding water on yourself," I answered, laughing. It had been a terribly painful experience for him when he was seven years old. Now, we could both laugh about it.

"Oh man!" Wayne exclaimed. "You're going to put **that** in there?"

I had to! I told him. It was too memorable to omit! I will never forget that day. Mama told the two of us to wash up a few dishes that were left in the sink. Wayne, ever the athlete, was in a big hurry to get finished so that he could get back outside to a football game with our young uncles and cousins, already in progress. He had been playing with them before Mama called us inside. She left us in the kitchen to go next door, to our grandmother Tiny's house. Before leaving, she warned us to finish our chore before going back outside.

We got busy, Wayne washing and me rinsing and putting the clean dishes into the dish rack. There was one pot left on the top of the stove. It was full of hot, steaming water. The thick vapors hung about the top of the pot like milky clouds.

Wayne went over and began trying to lift the ominous pot off of the stove. "You'd better wait until Mama comes back and let her pour that out," I warned him. We both saw that the water was still bubbling!

"I can do it," he said, both of his hands reaching for the pot. "I'ma hurry up and finish so I can go back outside!" He grasped the pot handles with his bare hands and lifted it from the hot eye. Before either of us knew what was happening, the handles slipped out of Wayne's hands and the pot tipped backwards! The angry water leapt onto his stomach, saturating his thin tee-shirt and denim shorts! Wayne screamed out in agony and dropped the pot on the floor. He began stripping off his clothes! The rest of the water that had not already been spilled, spat out at the floor around his feet! I watched him, my mouth wide open! He was jumping around in circles, trying desperately to get out of his shorts, tearing off his shirt!

I didn't realize that my brother was really hurt. I thought he was just clowning around, as he had been known to do quite regularly. Thinking that this was another one of those times, I began to laugh. "I'm gonna go and tell Mama," I cried, still laughing. I turned and ran out of the kitchen, out of the house. I left Wayne, still jumping around in the kitchen, and went next door to Grandma Tiny's house.

Mama and Grandma were in the kitchen, talking. They didn't seem to notice me coming in. When Mama turned around, I was sitting, poised on a stool, my elbows propped up on the counter, my chin resting in my hands.

"What are you doing over here?" she asked, putting her hands on her shapely hips.

I was about to answer, taking a moment to sigh dramatically.

She didn't give me the chance to. "You all better have those dishes washed when I get back over there!"

With as much articulation as I could muster, I said, "Mama, you ought to see Wayne!"

Mama wasn't interested in my drama. "He'd better be doing what I told him to do!" she snapped, obviously not amused.

"He was," I explained, "until he poured that hot water on his stomach and--"

Before I could complete my sentence, Mama screamed and ran out of the back door, Grandma on her heels! They rushed over to our house to find Wayne, down to his Fruit of the Looms, writhing on the floor in obvious agony! When I found out how badly he was hurt, I felt awful about having laughed at him.

Because of the third degree burns on his stomach, Wayne ended up having to repeat a grade in school. That didn't, however, lessen his love of sports any! He always has and still does love football! We have often laughed about his football "addiction" and the injuries he sustained trying to get a "fix!" On one occasion, he crawled under a house in order to retrieve the ball and keep the game going. When he emerged from beneath the house, he had cut his hand at the wrist! Crimson blood ran down his arm, but he still held onto the ball! Another time, he was playing with a group of boys in a wide vacant lot that everyone called "Dead Man's Valley" and he knocked himself unconscious in an attempt to catch the ball! He had run for a long pass, caught the ball, and turned to run for a touchdown, but was cut short by a forty-year old oak in centerfield! We took him to the hospital and they kept him overnight. Although he had talked to us immediately after the incident, Wayne told us the next day that he didn't even recall seeing us! The only thing he could remember was looking up and seeing that old tree!

Sometimes, I sit and look through some of the numerous photo albums we have laying around the house. I have accumulated quite a few pictures throughout the years, but we still have three large albums that my mom assembled when we were children. Sometimes, Tjai looks at pictures of me and my brothers and asks what our ages were in some of the snapshots. Amazingly, I can remember and tell him with such ease. On one picture, I am standing in front of the mirror, combing my headfull of hair. Wayne is seated in a big, green armchair, his legs gaped wide to expose a huge split in his pants! Michael is standing on Wayne's left, smiling what I have come to refer to as his "wide Clayton smile!" Ronnie is seated on the floor on Wayne's other side, looking as pleased as punch! We look like very happy children, not like four kids who had lost their parents less than a year before the snapshot was taken. We all appear happy and well-adjusted.

That picture was taken when I was almost nine years old. As a matter of fact it was taken by my cousin, the pervert! He was baby-sitting for Aunt Meg on one of the numerous times she had left us in his care. He was a popular football star at his high school. He spent much of the time he was supposed to be watching us, on the phone, talking to his many girlfriends. As I look at the picture and remember how unhappy and despondent I felt on the inside, I marvel at my ability to smile for the camera! Today, I stare at the photograph amazed at the little girl who was me. My heart and mind realize that something or someone was holding me, keeping me sane, helping me to cope. How else could I have survived? There is no other explanation. God has held me in the hollow of His hands all my life! I can say that beyond a shadow of a doubt. I am still here... because He still **is**!

"Keep me as the apple of the eye, hide me under the shadow of thy wings, From the wicked that oppress me, from my deadly enemies, who compass me about."
Psalm 17:8-9

After my secret was out and everyone knew that I could play the piano, my brothers discovered their own musical abilities! One Christmas, Aunt Meg bought Wayne a drumset and Michael a guitar. We became an ensemble! Ronnie didn't have an instrument, but he yelled as loud as the rest of us during our many impromptu performances -- which would usually take place when Aunt Meg was away from the house! She couldn't stand the noise we made, no matter how wonderfully talented we believed we were! As soon as her car pulled away from the house, we would go at it for all we were worth! We would sing the latest Aretha Franklin hit or Marvin Gaye tune. I belted out "R-E-S-P-E-C-T! Find out what it means to me!" at the top of my lungs, unaware that God was giving me yet another gift. Even in my pubescent screechings, He was anointing my voice!

When I was about twelve years old, I sang in the youth choir at our church. Around that same time, I became the youth choir musician. Now, in my opinion, I didn't play well at all! I would sit at the piano, as stiff as a board, my arms awkwardly stretched out in front of me and my eyes glued to the hymnal or piece of sheet music, whichever the choir was singing from. It was a real challenge, playing while someone was singing! I stumbled miserably, at times, but everyone always told me how beautifully they thought I had done. I smiled nervously, knowing that they were only being kind to me. God and I both knew I sounded horrible!

I seemed to do better when I played at home alone. Those times became less and less frequent though. Every time someone came to visit at our house, Aunt Meg would proudly announce to them, "I'll have Denise come and play something for you!" She was so proud of my musical talent. I cringed every time I heard her call for me to come and play. I would enter the living room where the upright Cote sat against the wall, sit down and open my piano book to the easiest piece I knew. I would play almost errorlessly, having already memorized the piece. Behind me, I could feel Aunt Meg beaming! After I finished, our guest would almost certainly applaud or say something clever like, "You've got yourself one fine musician there!" Only after that, would I be excused to return to whatever I had been doing prior to my recital.

It seemed that I spent a lot of time alone. At times, however, I played football with my brothers... when they'd let me, that is. I climbed trees with the best boys in the "hood." I also participated in games of "Cowboys and Indians" with as much enthusiasm as the next rambunctious boy on our street. I was clearly a tomboy, but I didn't mind the reference. After all, I had no sister to play with and there were few girls in our neighborhood. You could count them on one and a half hands. I knew them, played with them on occasion, but most of the time, I played with the fellows! Other than that, I pretty much kept to myself during the first year or so after Mama died.

When I discovered that God had given me a voice, it was as if a whole new world had opened up to me. That might sound cliché, but that is exactly how I felt! Once I opened my mouth and heard myself actually sing, I was excited! I really sounded like somebody! Oh, not anyone in particular, but I sounded like somebody! When I got started, I couldn't stop! I sang all the time -- while I was folding towels, mating socks, washing dishes or whatever! I sang in the kitchen and in the backyard! I even sang at night, in the tiny, cramped room where the four of us slept. At first, my brothers let me sing them to sleep. It was something our real mother had done many, many times while she was still with us. I thought I was filling in for her, in her absence. So, I sang to them, "Hush little baby, don't say a word; Mama's gonna buy you a mocking bird..." They went to sleep, my melodic voice softly ringing in their ears. "Unfortunately, after a while, that melodic voice began to get on their nerves!

"That's enough!" Wayne told me one night, just after I had gotten wound up. "Just let us go to sleep!" He yawned drowsily.

I was quiet, but offended. They didn't need me anymore, I thought. They didn't need Mama anymore. I still needed her. Why didn't they? I wondered. I stopped serenading them to sleep. I tried to go to sleep, trying to conjure up Mama's face into my mind. I wanted to see her, to look into her hazel eyes, to feel the warmth of her smile and the comfort of her touch. I missed Mama. Aunt Meg was a good guardian, but she wasn't Mama. I needed Mama, but even I knew that she was gone... forever.

I didn't sing to my brothers at night anymore, but I kept on singing. After one Thanksgiving dinner, I stood over the kitchen sink at our house on Twenty-Second Street, belting out a song, at the top of my lungs, as I had been known to do. My brothers were in Aunt Meg's room, sitting on the floor, watching television. Louder and louder, I sang until finally, I heard Wayne shout, "Will you please be quiet! We can hardly hear the T.V.!"

"That's okay," I retorted. "One day, people are going to **pay** to hear me sing!" I continued singing, but a few decibels lower.

"O Come, let us sing unto the Lord: let us make a joyful noise to the rock of our salvation." Psalm 95:1

In 1978, at age twenty, I left home and moved to Atlanta, Georgia. There were conflicting opinions as to why I did that. Without warning, I withdrew from college in Columbus and went north in search of greener pastures. I was optimistic! My mom was very upset that I had dropped out of college, for the second time! She insisted that I finish what I had started for once in my life and get my degree. She was very concerned about what others -- namely, her friends -- would think about my abrupt and seemingly irresponsible actions.

I was rebellious! I could have cared less what her friends or anyone else thought! It was my life and I was determined to live it anyway I saw fit! So, I packed my things into my popsicle blue '77 Mustang II and headed to "Hot-lanta!" Before I left, Aunt Meg made me promise that if I did not land a job within two weeks, I would come back home. I readily agreed, confident that I would get a job in Atlanta.

Being in what I then considered to be the "big city," I was filled with excitement and wonder! It was great to finally be out on my own! After a brief stay with my aunt, Margie, and her family, I had earned enough money to get my first apartment! I was ecstatic, moving in with very little furniture and a truckload of enthusiasm! It was a tiny, but cozy, one-bedroom apartment, about five minutes away from Aunt Margie and Uncle Leonard's house. I felt that I was far away enough from my family to maintain my independence, yet close enough, just in case I needed familiarity.

My boyfriend at the time, Isaac, was in Chattanooga, Tennessee, attending the same college where my brother, Wayne had gone on a football scholarship. It was less than a two-hour drive away. My Mustang II and I climbed the northern Georgia hills to visit him at every opportunity. When I didn't go there, he came to see me in Atlanta. I had been dating him since graduating from high school. I had found security, not only in him, but in his family, as well. Over the years, his mother became more like a mother to me than Aunt Meg had been at times. In that little apartment, I found a lot of time to sit and think about that. I was very close to Mrs. Ward. I told her a lot of things I had never shared with Aunt Meg, or anyone else, for that matter.

One afternoon, after I had begun writing, Mrs. Ward stopped by my house to see me. She had read both of the newspaper articles which reported the incident at school and my having found a sister, as a result of the first publication. When I opened the door, I saw a look of concern on her face. She was worried that the recent series of events might trigger some memories that might possibly be too painful for me and she wanted to be sure that I was faring well. I was amazed to hear her say that because that was exactly what was happening to me. I should have known that if anyone had any idea of what was going on inside of me, Mrs. Ward would be the one.

She had known about my past because we had talked about it, although superficially. Mrs. Ward reminisced about an incident which occurred one night as we were talking, sitting at her kitchen table. Isaac was not at home, but I was just visiting with her, one of hundreds of times. She recounted how, upon hearing gunshots being fired outside in front of her home, I suddenly sprang up and dove underneath the small, round table for protection! She said she had laughed at the time, but now, she realized that my reaction had been so dramatic because the gunshots had had a traumatic effect on me. It was a sound I well-remembered! Somewhere inside of me, the sound aroused panic and fear which I could not explain. I sought safety beneath that table, just as I had sought safety beneath the sofa bed in Grandmama's house on Baldwin Street! My reaction was instinctive. Before I realized it, I was crouched on the floor!

As she talked, a warm tear rolled down my cheek. "I didn't come over here to make you cry," she said, softly, in that motherly way she still has of speaking to me. "I just came over to make sure you were all right." She put her hand over mine, folded in my lap.

"I know," I said, wiping the solitary tear away. "I haven't even cried before now."

"I know it," she said. Then she added, "You really have never cried."

Immediately, I understand what she meant. I never really did cry. Of course, I cried at my mother and grandmother's funeral. I cried when Michael came home from the hospital. Through the years, I cried when I lost loved ones. I cried when I was happy. I cried when I was sad. But I never really cried about all the stuff-piled-upon-stuff in that room which had been suddenly pried open.

97

I really began to cry when I wrote about that awful night in November, 1966, when my life was changed forever. I cried because I realized that the door was really open and I would not be able to close it until all of the stuff had been unpacked and hopefully, discarded. That is what I'm doing... unpacking -- so that I can throw out all of the garbage and the shame -- once and for all!

"Therefore if any man be in Christ, he is a new creature: old things are passed away; behold, all things are become new." II Corinthians 5:17

The worse time to begin anew is before real closure takes place! When I met Travis, Tjai's biological father, I was an emotional mess! I had recently asked God to remove Isaac from my life because although I thought I truly loved him, I felt that I cared too much for him for my own good! Any and everything he did literally broke my heart! It was too much for me and so I prayed that God would put some space between him and me so that I could get some kind of control over my life. I really didn't think that He would move so quickly! Before I realized it, Isaac and I were history and I was devastated! When I had asked, I wasn't actually prepared to deal with it! I have since warned many people to be careful what they ask God for. I have learned that He does things in His own time, which may or may not necessarily coincide with ours! In any event, I asked and He delivered, promptly! Afterwards, I plummeted headlong into a state of depression.

A very good friend and co-worker, wanting to get me up out of my slump, thought it would be a good idea for me to start seeing other people. She cheerfully arranged a "blind date" between me and a friend of her husband's. We talked on the telephone and agreed to go out on Friday night. His car was being repaired so we agreed that I would come to his house to pick him up. We were going to go out for dinner and drinks.

I drove to a "ritzy" condominium community in northeast Atlanta to pick up my "blind date." I parked my Mustang in front of the address Travis had given to me and went up the stairs to the front door. I rang the doorbell. Travis opened the door. He was a tall, pecan tan-complexioned, attractive young man with slanted eyes framed by long, thick lashes and dark, wavy hair. A dark silky mustache rested above his wide smile. When I met Travis, I felt that there was something vaguely familiar about him, but I couldn't quite put my finger on it. Briefly, I spoke to his parents and then he and I left to go out for the evening.

We went to the Omni, to a small, intimate pub Travis liked to frequent. I can't recall the name of the place, but it was very quaint and quite charming. I wasn't looking for anything to come out of our arranged encounter, but he was nice looking and seemed more than outgoing enough. In fact, he was downright aggressive! He immediately "took charge" of our date, ordering a Long Island Iced Tea for me. I seldom indulged and had had difficulty deciding upon a cocktail, so he suggested I try one. Since I was not at all familiar with any of the drinks listed on the colorful menu, I didn't object to his recommendation.

When my drink arrived, I sipped it consistently. The taste was unique and the tea-colored liquid was smooth on my tongue. It was not long before I had finished it. Travis quickly summoned our waitress, who appeared to know him quite well, and ordered another Tea for me. We laughed and talked as we waited, nibbling from a basket of popcorn which had been placed on the table between us.

Very shortly, my second drink arrived. Travis was so funny and the more I drank, the funnier he became! In essence, I got wasted! I don't know when it happened, but I knew that it had when I got up to go to the ladies' room and the floor moved beneath my feet! I held onto the wall and tiptoed to the restroom. I could hear Travis laughing as I slowly made my way to the door.

By the time we left the pub, I was extremely intoxicated! I dropped my purse in the middle of Peachtree Street, just outside of the Omni, and I didn't even know it! Luckily an honest young man on a bicycle was passing by and noticed that I had dropped it.

"Hey, Lady," he called out to me, "you dropped your purse!" As his bike came to an abrupt halt, he reached down, retrieved it and handed it to me.

"Thanks," I said, sluggishly, taking my purse from him.

Travis had drunk even more than I had, yet he was still able to drive. I remember thinking that he drove like a maniac! At the time, I attributed it to his and my own intoxication! Later, I discovered that he drove like a maniac all of the time! Alcohol had absolutely nothing to do with it! He was so reckless behind the wheel of a car, I was a nervous wreck anytime I rode with him! I don't know if he thought he was a "daredevil" or some kind of stuntman or what! He just love taking risks on the road and seemed to get a rush from performing some fancy technique which, more often than not, resulted in skidmarks on the pavement! I hated to ride with him and insisted upon driving whenever fate tossed us into the same vehicle together!

I used to think the devil was after me. Now, I know it! He has been after me for a long, long time! I know this because of the incredible things that have happened to me in my lifetime. I can look back at some of the things that have happened to me and almost see Satan, licking his chops because he thinks he is just about to nab me! Then, to my surprise and his utter dismay, God or His angels would swoop down to rescue me! This has happened to me many times. I didn't even know it, until now. God has been watching, even at times when I wondered if He knew what I was going through. He has always been just a prayer away.

One evening I was talking to a friend, Clarice, and I expressed this revelation to her. That was the first time I had actually verbalized it, even though the thought had crossed my mind several times before. I remembered having discussed it with a minister I have known since I was twelve years old. I told Clarice that at the time, I had been living in Los Angeles and I was really going through some trials and tribulations. I had been playing for a church there and I had been propositioned by the pastor, whom I had had the utmost respect and admiration for. I had given him Father's Day cards and his wife had been like a sister to me. His children had taken piano lessons from me. I had found a place in their family and being with them had made home seem not so far away for me.

One Sunday, I didn't go to church because I was very sick with the flu. Tjai was just a toddler then. He was sitting on the floor, in front of the television. Unannounced, the pastor dropped by to see me. There was really nothing unusual about that because he and his family had been to my apartment on numerous occasions. This time was different though. During his visit, he became very aggressive and tried to kiss me. I was appalled! My face red with anger, I insisted that I could not and would not take part in what he was attempting to do! He told me that he understood, but continued his attempts nonetheless! The second time, I pushed him away and demanded that he leave!

Tjai never once took his eyes off the television. He didn't think anything strange about the pastor being there. Tjai felt like he was "family," too! After the minister finally got the message that I had absolutely no interest in an affair with him, he left. I never told his wife. I could not bring myself to hurt her like that! I loved her like a sister! I still do! I have never looked at him in quite the same way though.

After the incident, I called Rev. Davis, a trusted friend whom I had known since I was thirteen. Rev. Davis lived in Columbus. I told him about what had transpired and expressed my confusion about it. I could not, for the life of me, understand why something like that had happened to me! I told him that I had been trying to do what I thought was right and I had a very hard time trying to understand why someone I trusted in and confided in would do something like that to me! Rev. Davis, who always seemed to know just what to say and how to say it, told me that the devil was after me. I didn't know what he meant then. Now, I do. Like I say, he has been hot on my trail for a long, long time.

A few days ago, another minister said the same, exact thing to me. He told me that he had read the stories in the newspaper and from the little he knew about me, he recognized that Satan had been trying to get his hands on me. I told him that my life had been nothing short of miraculous! We both agreed on that! He told me that he believes that God has great works in store for me and he also knew that Satan was angry because for a long time, he had tried, unsuccessfully, to get his claws into me! He failed, time and time again, because God has something more for me. I am convinced that God's Will will prevail in my life. I have come too far now!

After a tumultuous courtship, I married Travis. It was really a ridiculously spontaneous thing to do. In fact, it was something a very unstable person would do. That unstable person was me. The moment I consented to marry him, I knew I had made a horrible mistake. Unfortunately, I didn't have the courage to admit it. Instead, I went ahead with plans for a simple wedding ceremony at our family church in Columbus in December of 1982. As the date drew nearer, I became more and more apprehensive about the event. Still, I said nothing.

On our wedding day, I was late getting to the church because I had a terrible stomach ache. I laid across the bed in my ivory lace wedding gown while my husband-to-be and our guests waited for me to walk down the aisle at the same church where my mother and grandmother had been funeralized sixteen years earlier. My heart already knew what my stomach tried to tell me. I was making a huge mistake! I didn't love Travis. I knew it and I believe that he knew it, too! I was his, on the rebound from the breakup of my relationship with Isaac. My heart still ached for Isaac as I walked up the aisle to be married to Travis. That day, as I faced him at the altar, my mouth made promises which my heart would never be able to keep. Ironically, the minister who performed the ceremony neglected to get around to the vows, so we never got to say them -- including the part that included "till death us do part." I noticed that he had skipped over those words, but I never mentioned it. He merely gave a brief synopsis on the State of Matrimony and then asked us if we each took each other into it. We both said we did and he proclaimed that we were husband and wife.

Two weeks later, I did one of those prodigal son numbers -- I came to myself! I realized my mistake and admitted to myself that I must end the farce before things went too far. I went to

Travis and confessed to him that I did not love him like a wife should love her husband. I told him that I believed that we had made a terrible mistake. I suggested that we get an annulment so that he could find someone to love him like he deserved to be loved. I thought he would see things from my point of view because I believed that, in his heart, he already knew. One evening, over dinner, I sat across the table from him and brought up the subject. As honestly as I could, I admitted to him that I had made a mistake and I felt it unfair to both of us to stay in a marriage which was obviously not entered into for the right reason. It made perfect sense to me and I actually thought he would be able to understand. To my surprise, he responded to my sincere confession with a threat upon my life!

"Before I let you go," he said, calmly, "I'll lay you down."

"What do you mean by that?" I asked, a confused expression on my face. I didn't really have to ask though. I already knew what he meant. He never responded because he knew that I understood him, all too well! He would kill me if I tried to leave him. I would die, I thought, probably at or around the same age my mother was when she died, twenty six! I was twenty-four years old then. In the next year that passed, I would see myself in my dreams, cold and dead like Mama, shot dead in the prime of my own life, by a man who didn't look like my father, but was him, just the same! I became terrified of him and he knew it!

My life became very empty and desolate. With each new day, I found that I resented Travis more and more! As the days passed, he became more and more rash, ill-natured and irrational. He was in and out of jobs, throwing temper tantrums and walking off from them when things did not go the way he thought they should. He was a professional chef and easily landed jobs at numerous four star hotels, only to quit at the slightest qualm. He began to drink excessively, and he would invite his drinking buddies over to drown their troubles in the same keg of beer with his! It was not unusual for me to come home from work, at the end of a long day, and find them sprawled out all over my living room in a drunken stupor. On one occasion, I walked in on Travis and two of his friends hovering over the dining room, as thick as thieves! As I approached them, I recognized thin lines of cocaine sectioned off on the glass table top. One of his friends was "snorting a line." Travis' eyes were glassy and his language was very slurred. I asked him, point blank, just what they thought they were doing. I knew that the white powder was cocaine, because I had seen it before. I was incensed that he was home, getting high, while I was out working all day!

I hated that he drank and used drugs! I despised his laziness and abusiveness! I hated that he wanted no more out of life than to hang out with people who wanted even less than he did! The void inside me had grown even larger. Travis did not love me. I knew he could not. He just wanted to possess me. I was like a rare bird he kept in a cage. I was a jewel he like to display. That's what Mama had been to Tony. I was Mama, reincarnated! I knew that I would never be able to love him and love was something I really wanted and needed! I needed someone to love. Convinced that there was no way out of the bed of thorns I had made for myself to lie in, I deliberately set out to get pregnant. A baby! That would definitely give me someone to love and someone to love me! It became my secret mission! I was convinced that I needed a child!

When I became pregnant with Tjai, I was overjoyed! Immediately, I stopped letting Travis touch me. When he climbed into the bed next to me, I either pretended to be asleep or I got out of bed altogether, went downstairs, and slept on the sofa. I didn't want him to touch me because I had come to despise his touch! He cursed that I had only used him to get pregnant. I didn't say anything, but it was true.

As I watched my stomach expand, I became exhilarated! Finally, I would have someone to love! I looked forward to the birth of my child with great anticipation. Travis saw a noticeable difference in me. I was happier, more content. He began to act very cruelly towards me. I already knew that there was no love in our relationship, but I realized that I was married to a man whom I knew did not love me and whom I had grown to hate! It was a miserable situation. He didn't love me, but I guess he felt the same way about me that Tony felt about Mama... if he couldn't have me...

I was four months pregnant when Travis beat me. That was the first and only time he did that. After he had used my body to demolish our new coffee table, I told him that one of us would die before I let him put his hands on me again! *Sophia* would quote me years later to *Miss Celie*. I think Travis believed me because he didn't hit me again. Instead, the mental torture commenced!

Travis' threats became a part of our daily conversation. Many times, I pulled back the covers on the bed we shared to find sharp, shiny butcher knives tucked beneath my pillow. Several times during the night, I would awaken to find him standing over me, staring down at me from cold, hard eyes. Years later, I realized that he did that to make and keep me afraid of him... too afraid to leave him. He knew about my past and my mother's fate. He knew that one of my deepest fears was of sharing that fate. He used my fear to keep me there, with him. And I stayed...for a while.

When Tjai was eight months old, God opened the door and let me ease out with my son and my life! I took my little angel and ran like a caged wild animal that had just been set free! I ran away from Travis and away from Atlanta! I put the miserable existence which had been my marriage to him in the room with Tony. I piled it on top of my childhood molestation. I covered Aunt Meg's cursing and criticism with it. I couldn't deal with it, so I simply got rid of it the best way I knew how... out of sight - - out of mind! Isn't that what they say?

Before I met Travis, I had a dream, but I had forgotten about it until long after I had left him. It was a dream about an alien invasion. Everyone had fled to safety, except me. I had been asleep and, as a result, got left behind. When I woke up, everyone had gone and the world had been invaded by large, monstrous, square-headed creatures. The creatures had oriental-looking eyes and thick, dark, wavy hair on their oversized heads.

In my dream, I ran to hide in a closet, hoping and praying that they wouldn't find me. One of the creatures opened the door to my hiding placed and I gasped for breath! My heart raced wildly and I opened my mouth to scream, but no sound came out! I woke myself up. I remembered the creature who stood towering over me in front of the closet door. I never told anyone before, but the creature looked just like Travis! That was possibly the reason he had seemed so familiar to me. I had seen him before I actually met him. God had shown him to me in my dream. He had confronted me, in that room that was my closet!

Since January, 1996, I have been singing with a gospel music ensemble. We always have prayer before beginning our weekly rehearsals. The leader of our group always asks God to "let no uncertain dangers come upon any member of the group" as he prays for our strength in the Lord. Each time I hear him say that, it reinforces my belief that God truly does watch out for us, His children! He warns us when danger is near. Sometimes, we take heed and sometimes we don't. Sometimes we just don't pay close enough attention! Satan takes advantage of those opportunities to "trip us up!" He is always somewhere, waiting for his opportunity. That is why God has told us to "watch and pray." Revelation is kind of scary, but what you don't know **can** and **will** hurt you!

"Weeping may endure for a night, but joy cometh in the morning." Psalm 30:5b

Since I began writing about my own revelation, I had become very nervous about the whirlwind of events going on around me. I had just finished writing about *Tony's last stand.* I got up from the computer and shut it down. I had about thirty minutes to get ready to go to my youth choir rehearsal that Saturday morning. I went into the bathroom to take a bath, trying to calm the flutter of nerves that had risen up in my stomach. I took off my clothes and stepped into the bathtub as the hot water poured from the faucet. I sat down, emerging my trembling body in the water and reached for the soap. I laid back in the water and breathed deeply, having just finished writing about what I know was the most difficult experience I had written about yet. Aloud, I asked God to give me the strength to deal with it.

"Lord, help me," I prayed, my voice bouncing off the walls in our small bathroom. "Help me to deal with all of this!" I hoped that He was listening. "Please Jesus, helped me to rise above it!" I prayed.

Before I could utter another word, my two year old, Christopher, pushed open the door. He was notorious for coming into the bathroom whenever he heard running water. Chris loves to take baths! He could have just had one, but if someone began running their bath, he usually appeared and began undressing so that he could get back into the tub. He came into the bathroom, right after I had asked God to help me rise above the weight and the pain of the past and to my amazement, he sung, in perfect pitch, "I bedeeve I can fwy! I bedeeve I can touch the sky!"

Chills spread across my entire body! It was as if God had heard my plea and was giving me His blessed assurance that I would, indeed, rise, somehow, through the tragedies of my past! Chris had heard that song numerous times as he watched one of his favorite videos, "Space Jam." He had listened to the song, penned and performed by pop artist, R. Kelly, over and over again. To hear my little precious baby boy sing those words to me, just at the exact moment I had made a prayer request known to God, was a miraculous thing! His tiny voice spoke boldly to me. His words gave me something I desperately needed -- hope! Christopher was the messenger and the message was from God!

"Out of the mouth of babes and sucklings hast thou ordained strength because of thine enemies, that thou mightest still the enemy and the avenger." Psalm 8:2

Six

In December, 1990, I got a glimpse of something I had hoped I would never see again...someone dying. This time, it was painstakingly slow. I would be given the opportunity to become even more familiar with its grim habits. Harry and I had been going to the nursing home every day -- sometimes, I went twice -- to visit with my mom. She had been at the facility for a little over a week. Her doctor, upon her release from the hospital, felt that she needed the attention that only a nursing home could provide. So she was moved to a facility not far from home to recuperate. Every day, I went to see her around lunch time. She would eat very little, but she seemed to be in a pretty good mood. Usually, she would make jokes with whomever was in the room with her. Sometimes, she recognized me and sometimes she didn't but always, I knew my mom, Aunt Meg.

I sat in a leather chair next to her bed and looked into and through the person she was rapidly becoming. In the nursing home, in the little room which she shared with an elderly white woman, Aunt Meg was out of her element. She looked out of kilter, lying helplessly in the narrow bed, instead of standing in the kitchen, over a casserole dish of oriental chicken.

It seemed that she was always in the kitchen, earnestly pouring over some recipe for at least twenty or more. For as long as I could remember, Aunt Meg had professionally catered for the entire city of Columbus. Her talents had spread her reputation as far north as Chattanooga, Tennessee, and as far south as Miami, Florida! Once, we all went down to the beautiful tropical city where she had been contracted to cater an anxious couple's wedding reception. How **they** had heard about her was beyond me. But there she would be, in the kitchen, doing what she did better than anyone else I knew -- cooking!

108

Aunt Meg cooked for people when they asked her to and when they did not. Some of her acquaintances would drop by our house unannounced just to see what she had cooking, hoping for a taste of some delicious morsel! Members of the city Fire Department had begun to look forward to Wednesdays when they would be privileged to partake of a brunch she voluntarily prepared for them. Quite often, my mom was rushing here and there with a freshly baked cake for someone, a loaf of Banana Nut bread for an elderly gentleman, whose name she did not even know, a piping hot dish of lasagna for someone who was feeling a little under the weather or cookies for a local boy scout troup. If it had been left up to her, no one would go hungry, not if she had anything to do with it! She loved to cook -- especially for those who loved to eat! She once told me that she was jealous of her other sisters, who had all been gifted with beautiful singing voices. Aunt Meg did not know what her gift was, but I knew. It was cooking!

I have often thanked God for providing more parents for us, after Mama and Tony died. But I have also wondered what He could have been thinking of. Nevertheless, Aunt Meg and Uncle Harrison willingly became "Mom" and "Dad" for the four of us. Interestingly, I never called them that to their faces. I still call my dad, "Harry."

My mom had a very wild sense of humor, even after she became ill with what I swore was Alzheimer's Disease. She had refused to teach me to drive, and having just turned fifteen, I was about to have a fit to get my learner's permit. After a lengthy lecture about responsibility, something she said I would undoubtedly never learn, she took me down to the DMV to get the first most important document I had ever received. When it was time for me to learn the "ropes" though, she assigned the task of teaching me to my dad. He was the calm, cool and collected one! After I "excitedly" hopped into the driver's seat, "conscientiously" turned the key in the ignition, "carefully" put the white 1978 Chevrolet Impala into reverse, "lightly" placed my foot on the gas and then "fervently" slammed backwards into a red dirt embankment across the street from our house on

Twenty-Second Street, my dad sat calmly across from me and said, very quietly, "Now, put the car in 'drive' and 'lightly' press on the gas."

I was so relieved. I knew if that had been Aunt Meg, it would taken me at least five more years to even get back behind the wheel of a car!

One Sunday, on the way home from church, Aunt Meg decided to let me drive. Needless to say, I was a nervous wreck! One wrong move and I knew my driving experience would be history! Sitting behind the wheel, I was very intent on keeping my eyes straight ahead on the road in front of me. We stopped at a red light and two teenage boys in an old beat up Chevy Nova pulled up beside us, on the passenger side. I was keeping my eyes straight ahead on the road, but I did notice them from the corner of my eye. To my surprise, Aunt Meg called loudly out of the window to the boys in the car.

"Hey! Hey!" she said. "This girl over here told me to tell you guys 'Hi!'"

I leaned forward in order to get a better look at them. One of them, the driver, was having a serious zit problem and the other one was missing a front tooth, which could be plainly viewed since he was smiling across most of his face! I felt my cheeks flush!

Aunt Meg began to laugh, almost hysterically!

Quickly, I returned my gaze to the traffic light, which by God's grace, was changing to green!

My relationship with my mom was not always that way. In fact, more times than not, I found myself at odds with her, trying to win her love and acceptance. For some reason, I felt that she did not really love me. She never said it, at least not until the last time I saw her alive.

I was not domestically inclined as a young girl. I think she wanted me to be more like her. I was more interested in other things like music, poetry, of scientific experiments or some kind or other. My mom used to say that she felt sorry for the man I was going to marry. I would respond, in my quip manner, that I had no intention of ever marrying anybody's son and then I'd go on about my business, banging on the piano or mixing up some generic concoction that was sure to set fire to the kitchen trash can... again.

I don't know when, but at some point, it became extremely important to me to have her love me like a daughter. I began to go out of my way to do things which I thought would help me to obtain that love. I would go on housecleaning sprees, working like mad to clean the house from top to bottom. Unfortunately, Aunt Meg always found something wrong with the way I did things. I never folded the bath towels quite the way she wanted them and the seams in my brothers' blue jeans were never quite straight enough. I even committed the ultimate housecleaning sin -- I dusted **before** vacuuming!

I don't know when I finally gave up, discovering that it was useless to try to win her over. I believed that she simply did not love me and nothing I could possibly do was ever going to change that! Another of my aunts told me that Aunt Meg had once told her that I reminded her of my real father, Tony. She hated him, too, and with good reason! He had not only killed my mother and grandmother, but they were also her sister and her mother! Aunt Meg thought that I looked like this man whom we both had significant reason to despise! Perhaps it was after I learned that that I stopped trying to please her and resolved to accept the fact that she would never love me like a daughter.

When I was a grown woman, with a child of my own, I told Aunt Meg how I felt. A very trivial matter incited a terrible argument between us. We were sitting in the den, watching television. I don't remember the program, but it was a musical. Smokey Robinson was singing and I began to hum along with him, "My mama told me, you'd better shop around..." Aunt Meg, seated on the sofa told me to "shut up" so that she could hear the television.

I was sitting on the floor and Tjai, who was thirteen months old at the time, was sitting in my lap. I stopped humming and looked up at her in amazement. I didn't say anything. I didn't even know what to say!

"I'm tired of feeling like a stranger in my own house!" she said, her voice cutting me to the quick.

I didn't know what on earth she was talking about, so I just stared at her, a look of confusion on my face.

She went on. "People think they can just come into your home and take over!"

Then, I knew. She was uncomfortable about Tjai and I being there. I had left Travis in Atlanta and sought refuge at home because I thought I could always come there when there was nowhere else to go. At once, I felt unwelcome in Aunt Meg's house. I didn't say a word. I simply got up from the floor, picked Tjai up and went upstairs. I went to my bedroom and put my son down on the bed. Then I took one of my suitcases from beneath the bed and laid it on the bed. It was time for us to go. I didn't have a clue as to where that might be, but I knew that it was time to leave.

She had followed me upstairs. She was standing in the doorway, looking at me, her arms folded across her chest.

I pretended not to notice her. I opened a drawer and began removing its contents, haphazardly placing them in the suitcase.

"What are you doing?" she asked. Her voice was razor sharp!

"I'm packing," I said, calmly. My stomach had begun to churn. I really didn't know what I was doing, but I kept doing it.

"Where are you going to go?" she asked.

What difference did that make to her? "Away from here," I answered, "so you can have your house back." I didn't even care that I sounded sarcastic.

She was silent.

"We don't have to stay where we're not wanted," I said, glancing at Tjai. He was playing with his shoestrings and making "baby" sounds. All the world was wonderful with him.

"I didn't tell you to leave," she said.

"You didn't have to." I kept packing.

"Well," she sighed, "that's just like you anyway!"

I didn't have any idea about what she meant by that, and I refused to ask.

She continued, "You never have needed anyone. You've always been **so** independent!" Now she was the one being sarcastic.

I snapped. "Like I had a choice!" I slammed the top of the suitcase down. "You were never there for me! I had no choice but to be independent!"

She looked at me incredulously, as if she didn't have a clue as to what I was talking about. I knew she must have.

I went on. "When I needed you the most, you weren't there for me!" I realized that I was yelling, but it was too late to go back now.

"You just have to have control of everything!" she said. "You come back here and just take over my house!" She was yelling now.

For a moment, I wondered if we were in the same argument.

"Your child picks up everything and has to touch everything!" she shrieked.

What did she think babies did? I knew she had never had a baby of her own, but surely, she had been around enough of them to know that they were curious creatures who touched and picked up things! I was offended that Tjai was now my child, as if he meant nothing to her! "Well, I guess Alvin is your child, because you sure don't seem to mind him touching your things!"

Alvin was my cousin's little boy. He was nine months older than Tjai. His mother had been brutally murdered by her jealous husband when he was only seven months old! He lived with my aunt, his grandmother. My mind went back to a few days earlier when Aunt Meg and I had gone to pick him up and bring him over to the house. Almost every day, she would go and get him and bring him over to play in the yard. She kept snacks, ice cream and candy around the house for him. That day, Alvin and Tjai were running and playing in the yard. Aunt Meg and I were sitting in lawn chairs, watching them. After a while, Aunt Meg asked Alvin if he wanted ice cream. Of course, he did. So did Tjai! Unfortunately, there was only one ice cream cone left in the freezer. In front of Tjai, Aunt Meg took it out and gave it to Alvin! I was really upset! I felt that if there weren't two, she should have left that one where it was! Tjai began to scream. I snatched him up and went inside the house to get my purse.

When we came back out of the house, we got into the car and I took him to the store for ice cream. When we got back, Aunt Meg and Alvin were gone.

Seething from the anger I recalled, I threw open the suitcase and began thrusting more clothes into it.

"Alvin doesn't have anyone else!" she said.

"He has a grandmother!" I retorted. "Tjai doesn't have anyone but me!" Tears began to stream down my face.

Then to my utter disbelief, Aunt Meg grabbed my arm, spun me around and slapped me across the face! I had not even realized that she was close enough to touch me! I was stunned, but I didn't have time to react! Her hand was raised to strike me again. She wanted to fight me! I grabbed both of her hands and held them out, away from me. By now, Tjai was screaming. He was obviously afraid! He slid down off the bed and rushed to us, forcing his tiny body between my mom and me. He wrapped his arms around my legs. Aunt Meg struggled to free herself from my grasp, but I would not let her go.

"I'm not going to fight you," I cried, "and I'm not going to let you fight me! I just left a prison where I had to fight just to stay alive! I'm not going to live in another one!" I was shouting!

Her struggling stopped abruptly. She stared at me. "What are you talking about?"

I was crying now, but I still held onto her hands. "I'm talking about living in fear! I'm talking about being afraid for my life! I have lived in fear ever since I married Travis," I screamed, "but you wouldn't know anything about that, would you? No! Nobody knew! Every waking moment, I was scared to death he would kill me -- or beat me so bad I wished I were dead!"

"Beat you--?"

"Yes! Beat me! He beat me when I was pregnant with Tjai! I thought he was going to kill me! He stood over me when I slept, making d---- sure that I was scared of him! He threatened to kill me! I didn't even think I would live this long!" I screamed.

Tjai was screaming, too.

Aunt Meg was silent now. Tears ran down her nut-brown face.

114

I went on, unable to stop the flood of emotions gushing out from my heart. "I had to stay there -- to live like that until God heard my cry and made a way for me to get away from that maniac! I prayed every single day for Him to help me to get away from him! And I came home because I thought I could come home when I couldn't go anywhere else! And for what?!" It wasn't a question. I wasn't really expecting an answer either. "For you to make me feel like I'm not welcome! Like we're not wanted here!" I shrieked. "Well, don't worry! We're not staying!" I released her hands and went back to packing, snatching open drawers and shoving clothes into the suitcase like a mad woman!

For a moment, Aunt Meg stood there silently, watching me. I guess she was trying to absorb the shock of all that I had just thrown at her. She had not known. But then, nobody had. I had told no one about the hell I had married into. I told no one about the abuse I had lived with. I had reasoned in my own mind that if I told someone in my family about what was going on, they might try to come to my assistance. My husband was my father, revisited! I could not endure a reenactment of the tragedy that had left me motherless! I wanted to be there for my son, to watch him grow, to touch him, to love him! I knew I couldn't do those things from a grave! So, I opened the door to the room where my father and his hideousness had been buried and deposited more painful memories there -- more stuff!

Her voice seeped into my mind, "Why didn't you tell me?"

The question was ridiculous! Why would I tell her? She had never been there for me. Why should I have told her?

"I didn't know you were going through all that," she said, her voice solemn.

"I know you didn't know," I sighed. I stopped packing and looked at her, standing in the doorway. She looked like the wind had been knocked out of her. "No one knew... but God."

Tjai and I stayed in Aunt Meg's house for about four more months. That's how long it took for me to work and save enough money to move to Los Angeles. In July, 1985, I really packed! I packed up my son and all of our belongings into a U-Haul trailer attached to my '84 Chevrolet Cavalier and headed west! I was leaving the pain behind, or so I thought. I was leaving Georgia, leaving home, leaving Tony, leaving Travis, leaving pain, leaving sorrow, and leaving that closet -- all behind! Los Angeles was on the other side of the world to me. It was far as I could go without getting my feet wet! I believed that none of that stuff would be able to reach me there. It was far enough away. What I didn't know was that I was taking it with me! All of it!

Tjai and I lived in Los Angeles for five years. In November, 1990, I drove the Cavalier back across the country and returned to Georgia. A week to the day we got back, Aunt Meg had a heart attack. For a month, she laid up in the hospital, moving in and out of the intensive care unit. In December, she was taken from the hospital to a nursing facility. I don't think she even knew where she was. She seemed to be on the mend. She had begun the road back to her old comical self. When I came in to her room, if she had company, she would have them in the bowls of hysterical with some antic or other. I was glad that she was getting better. Even though our relationship had never been what I had wanted it to be, I was still glad to be back home.

I promised myself that I would stay in Columbus, to care for her and Harry, until she was able to do it herself, no matter how long it took. I had already received a telephone call from a major communications company in Atlanta. They had a job offer for me. I was anxious to take it, but, as I explained to the nice woman on the phone, I had to take care of my parents first. Hopefully, the job would still be there for me after my family crisis was over. She said that they would keep checking with me and she offered her best wishes for my mom's recovery. In the meantime, I cleaned Aunt Meg's house, cooked for Harry, did the laundry, and visited the nursing home, twice a day.

The day after Christmas, 1990, I visited with my mom for most of the day. I found her sitting up in the bed, looking extremely radiant! When I walked in, she asked me if I would mind filing her nails. They had become quite ragged since her illness first began. I did that for her and then threatened to paint her toenails bright red with some polish that happened to be in my purse. she laughed, telling me that I had better not because she wouldn't want to shock anyone that much! I cannot ever remember her wearing any nail polish.

We laughed and talked a lot that day. I particularly remember something she said that still makes me laugh. The elderly woman who shared the room with my mom was bedridden. The pale, petite woman was crippled and could only get from her bed to the TV chair if she were carried. I had seen this done several times while visiting my mom. Aunt Meg was talking about Christmas having just passed and she complained that no one had given her a single, solitary gift. Realizing that she did not remember the previous day, I reminded her that I, along with at least fifteen other people in our family, had visited her on Christmas Day and brought her armloads of gifts. I walked over to the closet adjacent to her bed and opened it to show her the beautiful robes that we had given her. They were hanging neatly in the closet. She just said, "Oh," as if she had just remembered. Alzheimer's Disease has that effect on people. Sometimes they remember forty years ago much clearer than they recollect yesterday.

Aunt Meg began talking about her mother, my grandmother, as if she were still alive. That bothered me. She said that she was going to get some fresh collards and cook them for her mother as soon as she could.

"Aunt Meg," I said, as gently as I could, "Grandmama died a long time ago. Don't you remember?"

She looked at me through somber eyes and said, "Yes, I remember. I just didn't want to."

Those words gave me a strange feeling.

She went on to tell me of her plans to live in the house with her mother. In a serious, quiet voice, she made me promise to take care of Harry. That really shook me up! I didn't want to hear any talk about death or dying and I sensed the topic coming up. Quickly, I told her that I would take care of him until she came home, and I assured her that she shouldn't worry about anything except getting well! I conveniently changed the subject and she let me.

As Aunt Meg, the comedienne resurfaced, a sly expression crossed her face. "Did I get her something?" she asked, gesturing towards her roommate, who was engrossed in a television program.

I shook my head 'no.'

Aunt Meg squinted her bright, slanted eyes and appeared thoughtful. "I really should get her something," she said.

I shrugged. "What do you want to get her?"

Then she came up with what must have been the most hysterical thing I had heard in a long time. "Do you think she has a bicycle?" She burst into laughter and I literally laughed until I cried!

The next day, my dad and I went to see Aunt Meg, after work, as usual. The only difference was that this time, I had not taken Tjai with us. He was with relatives who had kept him for me during the day. When I walked into her room, ahead of my dad, I nearly gasped! The woman lying in my mom's bed was not the same person I had sat with, talked to, and laughed with the day before! Aunt Meg's radiant complexion had faded and the laughter I had seen in her eyes was gone! She was lying in the bed, physical restraints on both wrists.

I turned and rushed out of the room to the nurse's station. A very thin woman looked up at me over wire-rimmed glasses.

"May I help you?" she drawled in her thick Southern accent.

"What happened to my mother?" I asked, obviously upset.

"Mrs. Seagram?" she asked.

"Yes," I said. "She didn't look like that yesterday!"

"Oh, yes, I know," she said. "Let me get her nurse for you." She picked up the telephone on her desk.

I couldn't hear what she was saying, but in a matter of seconds, a male nurse approached me at the desk.

"You're Mrs. Seagram's daughter?" he asked.

"Yes," I answered. "What happened to her?"

"She fell earlier today," he explained.

"Why didn't someone call us?" I asked.

"We tried to call you and your father?"

118

"Where?" We had been at the shop all day long. No one had called us.

"Well," he continued, "she got out of bed and tried to leave the facility. That's when she fell."

I stared at him.

"We took her to the Medical Center to have X-rays, just to make sure she hadn't broken any bones or anything."

"Did she?"

"No ma'am. She was all right. When we brought her back, we had to restrain her so that she wouldn't try to get out of bed and possibly fall again." He ended his explanation and looked nervously at the woman at the desk. She had been watching us the entire time.

"Was she awake?" I asked.

"Ma'am?"

"When you brought her back, was she awake?"

"Oh, yes ma'am. She was fully conscious."

I looked down the hall, towards Aunt Meg's room. I realized that what had happened to her didn't happen during her fall. When she came back to the nursing home, she realized where she was. She was in a nursing home, a place she had told us she never wanted to have to go. When we were kids, she told us to never, ever put her in a nursing home. No matter what happened to her, we were to never let that happen. She believed that people who ended up there were often mistreated and ignored. She didn't want that to happen to her. I knew that, but I made random visits throughout the day to make sure that she wasn't being mistreated and we had no intentions of leaving her there to be ignored. She was to remain there just long enough to recuperate. After that, we had plans to take her back home.

At that moment, I was relieved that I had not brought my six year old son with me. On another occasion, she had been restrained and he had become very upset about it -- so upset that we had asked the nurse to remove the restraints as long as we were there. If Tjai had seen his grandmother in her present state, he would have been devastated! She was lying there,

119

limp, lifeless and exhausted! When Aunt Meg got of bed and fell that day, her body had not been broken, but it was evident that her spirit had!

She was staring up at a corner of the room, chewing on an apricot that had been part of her dinner. Her tray was still in front of her. I watched her chew for a few moments and then offered to remove it from her mouth. I picked up a napkin from her tray.

"Do you want me to take that?"

"Uh-uh," she said, not even taking her eyes off of the corner to look at me.

I put the napkin down.

She was fixated.

I looked up at the corner to see if I could see what she was looking at. I saw nothing. I looked down at her tray. She had eaten most of her food. I knew her nurse had fed her. Then, I noticed something which caused my heart to stir. Two empty milk cartons rested on their sides on top of her tray. It seemed very odd to me because I knew that my mom did not drink milk.

The male nurse entered the room.

I turned and looked at him. "Who drunk those?" I asked, pointing at the empty cartons.

"She did," he said, smiling.

I turned back to Aunt Meg, a look of despair crossing my face. Why would she choose now to start drinking milk? She was sixty-five years old! Something deep within me began to panic! I had heard many stories of people who, at the point of death, do things they don't normally do. Harry's mother, Grandma Seagram, who had been blind as long as I had known her, was sitting on her daughter's front porch the day before she died. Aunt Louise said that Grandma Seagram had asked her the strangest question that day. She wanted to know why they had not planted any green peas that year. How could a blind woman discern that no green peas had been planted? Could God have granted her her sight on her last day on earth? Did He let her see so that she could bid 'farewell' to His creation? I wondered. Why did Aunt Meg drink that milk?

We didn't stay long. She looked so tired. She looked gray, too. I didn't say anything to my dad about that, but she looked like a hologram to me, something gray and unnatural-looking. I suggested that we go on home and let her get some rest. I leaned close to her and kissed her on her forehead. Her skin felt cool. "We'll see you tomorrow," I whispered.

"Uh huh," she said.

"I love you," I said, stroking her hand.

To my surprise, she said, "I love you, too." She had never told me that before! In all the years I had dusted and vacuumed, washed and ironed, cleaned and re-cleaned, cooked and re-cooked, in search of her affection, she had never said those words to me! Although I had "lived" to hear them for what seemed like most of my life, now, upon hearing her say them, I had mixed emotions. At the door, I turned and looked at her one more time. She was still looking up at something in the corner of the ceiling.

That was the last time I saw Aunt Meg alive. In my heart, I guess I knew it would be, but my mind simply would not let me accept that. In fact, on the way home, Harry and I discussed the living arrangements that would have to be made for her when she was released from the nursing facility. She was scheduled to return home in a few days, something to do with Medicare requirements. Harry and I didn't know it, but Aunt Meg had other plans. When the telephone rang at one o'clock in the wee hours of the morning, I knew that those plans had been carried out, even before I answered the call.

It did not occur to me until much later that the last time I saw her alive was the first time she had ever told me that she loved me. Oddly, I had received it somewhat unceremoniously, as if I had always known.

"I will lift up mine eyes unto the hills, from whence cometh my help." Psalm 121:1

121

Tjai and I spent the first seven years of his life alone, together. I was not just mother, I was his father, sister, and brother, too. And he was everything to me! I talked to him about things that bothered me as if he were old enough to understand. He often sat and listened attentively to me. When he talked to me, he spoke with the wisdom of someone much older. I realized that he was talking to me just like I was talking to him. In some ways, we were equal. We were both trying to fill a void in our lives. I tried, however, to convince him that I was not trying to be his friend. I was his mother, the disciplinarian!

Although I encouraged Travis to establish some kind of relationship with Tjai, he never really did. It has been more than nine years now since they have seen each other. Tjai, of course, was only four years old then. I'm not sure he even remembers Travis. Before Darrell became a father to him, Tjai used to ask why his own father didn't call him or come to see him. I never tried to talk negatively about Travis, but I never "sugar-coated" the facts either. I explained to Tjai that some people fathered children, but that didn't make them fathers. Likewise, there are a lot of women, even teenage girls, who have babies, yet they are incapable of being or not willing to be mothers to their children. I tried to convince Tjai that I loved him enough for both his father and me. Although I told him that he should not worry about it, I am sure that he did. After all, he had friends who had fathers living in the home with them. Why shouldn't he have one, too? It took seven years, but God gave Tjai the father he deserved. He could not have found a better father than the one he got in Darrell.

I have concluded some things about life in general. One is that it is definitely too short to be wasted. Another is that we must do the best we can with the hand life deals to us. This is not a practice run. There is no rehearsal. We only get one and we have to live it to the fullest. That's why I left Travis. I had made a mistake and I saw no need to waste another day, another precious moment, another breath in a relationship that was doomed from the start! It made no sense to.

A couple of months after Tjai was born, I overheard Travis talking with one of his cronies on the phone. I thought my ears were playing a cruel trick on me when I heard him say that when his son was ready to try marijuana, he would be the one to introduce him to it! I was mortified! I could not believe my ears had heard something so utterly ludicrous! I was absolutely determined that he would never be able to introduce drugs of any kind to my son! I made a firm decision that before I let my son be raised by the "improper" male influence, there would be no male influence! So as soon as fate allowed, I took Tjai as far away from his biological father as I could go without jumping aboard an ocean liner!

"Then shall the lame man leap as an hart, and the tongue of the dumb sing: for in the wilderness shall waters break out, and streams in the desert." Isaiah 35:6

I made a conscientious decision to resign from my school system in April, 1997. I knew I could never return to that school. Too many things had happened... too much water gone under the bridge. I called the superintendent and told him that I would fax my resignation to his office on Monday. School was out for Spring Break. He told me that he would still be in the office to receive my fax, if I sent it Monday or Tuesday. Initially, I had planned to send him a one-liner, stating that I would not be seeking employment in the district for the next school term. By the time I got to Ophelia's office to send the fax to him, I had decided to go ahead and send him my resignation, to be put on the school board's agenda for their next meeting. I knew that they would have to receive it and vote to release me during their upcoming monthly meeting.

One of my former administrators, Mr. Edwards, dropped by to see me one Monday evening before the school board was to act upon my resignation. During our conversation, he made an observation about me which I felt to be very profound. He said that in the midst of the recent turn of events affecting my life, I had been beyond suicide. I looked at him curiously, not quite sure what he meant.

123

I remembered a Friday night, about three weeks earlier, when Darrell and I had gone to the grocery story. Our toddler, Christopher, had accompanied us. I had just met Debra and was still feeling overwhelmed by her sudden entrance into my life. When we pulled up in front of the store, I shuddered. "Aaugh!!" I said, my whole body shaking in the seat.

"What is the matter with you, Denise?" Darrell asked, giving me a frustrated glare. I guess he was becoming a little frazzled because I seemed to be more and more so lately.

I didn't even know where or how to begin to explain to him what I was feeling, so I just said, "Nothing."

He sighed. "Do you need anything?"

"No," I answered. "Just hurry." I was afraid to be left alone for too long.

Christopher was sitting next to me, playing with an action figure. I looked down at him. I needed to feel a presence greater than that he was capable of providing me at that moment. I watched his little fingers as he handled the toy, absorbed in his own little world, as my own came apart at the seams.

In a few moments, Darrell had returned. "Are you okay?" he asked, opening the door to get back into the car.

I was grateful he had made it back so quickly. "Uh huh," I lied. I was not okay. I did not even know when I would be.

As I sat and talked to Mr. Edwards, I finally figured out what he meant. I had been there. I told him so. It was like being on a cliff, all but jumping off. I wanted to jump off, but something would not let me. That something was my children. I could not let my children grow up without their mother! That had been my fate. I was determined that would never happen to my own children. I left Travis because I did not want Tjai to grow up without me! Fortunately, I did not succumb to the temptation of suicide because I knew that Tjai and Christopher needed me, their mother! As I listened to Mr. Edwards, that became increasingly clear to me.

He said that suicide was the result of hopelessness. People feel hopeless when they experience feelings of worthlessness.

He also told me that when people are out of work, they feel like that. I had been out of work, out of my classroom. I had not been able to go back to school and do what I loved doing. I also had not been able to sing like I wanted to since having had a Thyroidectomy last November. The muscles in my throat had not yet healed enough for my voice to return to full strength. So, I couldn't sing like I used to. Mr. Edwards sensed that teaching and singing had both provided a release for emotions which had been coming to a head within me. He agreed with me that this day had been coming for quite some time now.

Being faced with the threat of danger in the classroom triggered the emotions which I had suppressed for the past thirty years! That forced me out of the classroom environment, out of work. Finding myself unable to do what I had been used to doing, teaching and singing, and absorbing myself completely in both, I experienced what Mr. Edwards was talking about... that sense of worthlessness! I confessed to him that I had told Darrell, just a couple of weeks ago, that I felt like I had nothing. Darrell had not understood what I meant. In his opinion, I still had everything I always had. I was just temporarily out of the classroom and somewhere within me was my voice, waiting for the muscles in my throat to recover! But I felt that I had lost everything! I felt uselessness where I had once felt so much purpose for my existence!

Mr. Edwards also commented that he knew there was a "glue" that had held me together in the past two months. That glue was my husband and my children. His realization reinforced what I had already concluded... that God gave me what He knew I was going to need in order to get through this ordeal... a supportive husband and my children.

When I woke up the next morning, Mr. Edwards' words were still fresh on my mind. I remembered something he had said about my defenses having worn down, even before violence erupted in my classroom. He reminded me how sensitive I had become after returning to school from my surgery. He said the loss of my voice, though temporary, had weakened me. I laid in the bed and recalled a day, not too long before that my Senior class had expressed their desire to switch to the other English teacher at the end of the first semester. There were only two of us teaching English at the high school. They accused me of trying to prevent them from graduating because I expected them to actually learn something during their last year in high school! They didn't want to do any reading or writing. This was evident when only one person out of the entire class of thirty passed a test on a novel they had been assigned to read. I had given them two months to read Richard Wright's Native Son, but none of them actually read it. Some had rented the movie, but it was virtually impossible to write an essay on the one-question test, without reading the book. Everyone, with the exception of one person, made an "F" on the test! They were really teed off! They told me that they preferred to finish out the year with the other teacher. I already knew that the option to switch classes at mid-year was at our mutual discretion. I didn't tell my students that, however.

I stood at the podium in front of the class and stared blankly at them. I was hurt that they no longer wanted to be in my class. My body was rigid and my voice calm as I told them that I would speak to Mrs. Weisner concerning their request. "Maybe we can work something out between us," I said.

They went wild! They almost applauded!

I was crushed. "You may all go to lunch now," I said, calmly dismissing them. The students bounced cheerfully out of the room. I went to my desk and sat down in my chair. How could they not want to learn anything? I was devastated. For this, I came back to teach another year? What could I have been thinking of? I closed my eyes and tried to fight back the tears. After a few minutes, I composed myself and went to join my students in the cafeteria.

I was sitting at the table alone. The usual crowd was absent that day, so I had no one to talk to. My tray sat in front of me, but I was unable to eat a morsel. My heart was heavy, but I was determined not to fall apart. I was doing pretty well, until Mr. Edwards sat down at the table, opposite me.

"Mrs. Bryant!" he began, in his usual enthusiastic manner. "How are you today?" He took one look at my face and his enthusiasm dwindled. "What's the matter?" He put the notepad he had been carrying on the table.

I shook my head, "Nothing." I knew that if I tried to say anything more, I would not be able to control my emotions.

He looked at me. "Did someone do something to you?"

"No," I mumbled. I stared down at the food on the tray in front of me.

Mr. Edwards sighed. "Do you have a class right now? Where is your class?"

I motioned towards the group of students who were sitting at two adjoining tables nearby. I tried to explain to him what had happened my classroom. "They want to go to Mrs. Weisner for the rest of the school year," I said. "They think that I want to keep them from graduating. All I really want is for them to learn."

Mr. Edwards smiled. "I see," he said. "You just sit right here." He got up from the table. "I will take them back to class and keep them for you for the rest of this period. You go to the Media Center and relax, all right?"

I nodded. I glanced over at my students. Several of them were watching Mr. Edwards and I. I inhaled and exhaled a deep, cleansing breath.

"Get yourself something to read," he continued. "Or better yet," he took a copy of a newspaper article out from between the sheets of his notepad, "read this." He handed the article to me. "It will help you to understand a little better."

I took the article from Mr. Edwards and looked at it. It was about rural area schools and increasing failure rates. When I left the cafeteria, I headed for the Media Center. I found an empty conference room and went inside, sat down, and began to read. The kids in the article sounded very much like my students... most of them! The author of the article discussed the rising number of students who were failing, as well as some contributing factors. At the top of the list were the absence of family values, drug trafficking, gang involvement and teenage pregnancy. All of these conditions were met at my school.

Several of my students were undisciplined and disrespectful of authoritative figures, or any adult, for that matter. Some showed very little or no respect for their own mothers! How could I expect them to respect me? Some boasted of their gang affiliation, and I knew that they were involved in drug use and/or sale. One student had asked me to pick up a tri-board for a class project. In front of me, he took a wad of bills from his pocket and turned back at least five one-hundred dollar bills before taking out a twenty and handing it to me! To my knowledge, he didn't even have a job! Several of the young ladies in my class were pregnant, too! Two of my ninth grade students were expecting to deliver any time soon. I was reading about students in other parts of the country, but I recognized those I attempted to teach every day!

Mr. Edwards was right about one thing. After reading the article, I did have a better understanding! It wasn't that the students didn't want to learn from me. For an overwhelming number of reasons, they simply did not want to learn!

Later on, that same day, I discussed the students' request with Mrs. Weisner. At the same period in which they came to me, she had a small group of "at risk" students. They were some who had been socially promoted to the ninth grade after having been unsuccessful at getting there on their own at least two times. She often fondly referred to them as her "Bad News Boys." When I told her that my students wanted me to take her students so that they could switch over to her, she laughed.

"That's because they know you mean business and they don't want to do any work!"

"Well, I don't know what they expect me to do," I said. "They act as if they're just coming to school every day, taking it easy as they wait for graduation… like they don't need to know anything else."

"Well," she said, "little do they know, they need you more this year than any other year they've had!"

I knew she thought it was best for me to keep them. I thought so, too. I guess I just didn't feel like dealing with their resistance. I wasn't up to the fight. All my defenses were on their way down. Why deal with something I could avoid, for once? As much as I had looked forward to teaching those kids, I was willing to let them go. As fate would have it, Mrs. Weisner and I didn't switch. She kept her "Bad News Boys" and I kept my apathetic seniors, at least for the moment. To their eventual satisfaction, I ended up leaving the school.

After I had been gone for about a month, one of my sophomore students called me at home and told me that the seniors were glad that I was gone I wasn't surprised. They honestly believed that I stood in the way of their graduating. I told her that I knew they thought that. Unfortunately, I said, they felt that way because they knew I was serious about them learning something in my class during their final year of high school. What the students did not realize was that their only obstacle was themselves!

I attended the Tuesday night school board meeting. I knew they would be voting on whether or not they would accept my resignation and I wanted to be present, just in case something came up. Darrell and I sat patiently through a long, drawn out series of presentations from the principal and other school personnel. As I sat next to him, I looked over a copy of the meeting agenda and discovered that mine was not the only resignation the board would be acting upon at the meeting. To my surprise, there were two others! Towards the end of the meeting, the superintendent addressed all three resignations. When he called for a recommendation from the board, the members voted unanimously to accept my resignation, as well as the others. Another had been received that same day. They moved to address that one at a later date.

After the meeting, several board members wished me well in my future teaching career. I shook hands with those who smiled, somewhat sympathetically, and expressed their regret at losing me from the system. I thanked them for their support during my tenure with the system. A couple of them apologized to me for what had happened at the school. Other teachers and school personnel hugged me warmly and likewise wished me the best. If I didn't know any better, I would swear that my principal, who had been sitting directly behind Darrell and I, avoided me like the "plague." Darrell went out of his way to speak to him. As we left the Board Office, I told him that the principal had not said one single word to me.

"I went over and talked to him," Darrell said, unlocking the car door for me. "Hmmm," I murmured, getting to the car. I watched him go around to the driver's side. My husband sure was something when he wanted to be, I told myself.

Shortly after the school board met, I was offered a job in the system where I live. I had hoped to get a job there for the next school year, but things worked out -- or rather God worked things out -- so that I could get in before the current school year was over.

I went over to a local middle school to meet with my new principal, who had been an assistant principal at my high school when my brothers and I attended there. It was amazing to me that he looked much like he did when I was in high school! He remembered me and of course, he remembered my older brother, Wayne, the athlete! Mr. Braddock had been his coach at one time. He recalled that Wayne had been an all-star athlete and a very respectful young man. Everyone who knew my big brother loved him!

"How's Wayne?" Mr. Braddock asked, offering me a seat, across from his neatly organized desk.

"He's fine," I said, smiling. "He's living in Chattanooga."

"Yes," Mr. Braddock, "I knew that he had gone to school there. My wife's brother lives there, too."

"Well," I smiled, "He never came back to Georgia to live."

We talked briefly about "what," "who," "where," "how," and "why" of what I had been doing since high school and then we got around to discussing the job that had become available at his school. The position was for a Math and Science teacher, two subjects I had never taught before. I had taught in Middle School during my college student teaching experience, but I had not been in either of those fields. I felt confident, however, that if

Mr. Braddock wanted me to teach Woodshop, I would do my best to teach it! I wanted the job, desperately. I missed teaching! I needed to go back to the classroom! He showed me the textbooks and I leafed through them as he continued to talk about the position. It didn't look very difficult to teach pre-Algebra, and the Science textbook looked simple enough. After all, they were teacher's editions. All of the answers were in the book!

I assured Mr. Braddock that I could do a good job teaching. He looked at me as if he believed me, too. He told me that if I wanted it, the job was mine.

If I wanted it? More than anything, I wanted it! More than peace of mind, I wanted it! And I desperately wanted peace of mind! I don't think he knew what he did for me that day, but I will be eternally grateful to him and his administrators for giving me the opportunity to get back a portion the confidence and dignity that had been misplaced during my last teaching experience! I looked forward to my first day at the new school with enthusiasm and tremendous optimism. I knew it would be a challenge to teach out of field, but I didn't care about that. I was up to it! I would do what teachers should be doing anyway, not just teaching, but learning along the way!

It was Spring Break. The Friday before I was scheduled to begin my teaching assignment at the middle school, I took my boys and went over to fix up my classroom a little. I took some things I had used in my former classroom, along with a few new things. I wanted to put something inspirational on the bare eggshell colored walls. Environment has a lot to do with learning! If a classroom looks stimulating enough, kids will at least stay awake long enough for the teacher to stimulate them!

Mr. Braddock met me at the school to let me in and then he left for an appointment. Tjai and Christopher played with my poster putty so that it would be the right texture to secure my pictures to the concrete wall. While they were doing that, I was busy, selecting the pictures I would use and deciding where they would go. I decided to put pictures of the 1996 Olympians on the wall, along with a sign I had made. The sign read: "Olympian:

One who strives with heart, soul, body and mind to be the best!" I had come up with that definition at the start of the 1996-97 school year because for one thing, we had just celebrated the Summer Olympics in Atlanta. Secondly, I thought I could use the theme to motivate my students to aspire to be their personal best.

I had been told that my new middle school students were at risk because they had failed the seventh grade last year. The program I would be teaching in was called the "Step Up" program and it had been developed to help the students by giving them both seventh and eighth grade work during the school year. If they passed, they would go on to the ninth grade in the next school term. I would have very small classes. That suited me just fine! After having come from my last school, I knew that this new environment would offer me less stress. I would be back, doing what I loved to do... teaching!

The next day, Saturday morning, I woke up feeling anxious about the coming Monday. I was excited to get started. In an attempt to calm my racing heartbeat, I decided to lay in bed for a while, at least until after eight o'clock, just to relax. I couldn't. So, I bounced out of bed and went to the kitchen to get a cup of coffee. Tjai was already up, having made his own. Recently, both he and Christopher had decided that they needed to have their morning cup of coffee, so we bought a jar of decaf. He was pouring water into his cup when I walked into the kitchen.

"'Morning, Mom."

"Good morning," I said. "Is there enough water in there for me?"

"Yep!" he answered, setting the ivory kettle back down on the warm eye. He took his cup and went down into the den to watch T.V.

I fixed my coffee and a piece of toast. I walked into the dining room and sat down in a chair at the table. "Tjai, bring me the newspaper," I called to him.

He brought me the day's paper and sat down in a chair across from me. I was glad he did. There was something I wanted to say to him. "Tjai," I began, "do you know why your dad and I keep on you about doing your school work?"

He gave me his usual blank adolescent stare.

I continued anyway. "We do that because we want you to make good grades... for yourself. It's not for us, even though we're the ones fussing about it. It's for you. Do you understand that" I took a sip of my coffee and waited for him to respond.

"Yeah," he said, quietly. His expression told me that he was preparing himself for chastisement.

"Do you remember when I was in college, preparing to become a teacher?" I asked.

"Yes ma'am."

"Do you remember how I used to get up early and say up late studying?"

He nodded.

"Why do you think I did that?"

He didn't answer. He knew I would tell him.

"I did it for me," I said.

He was surprised at my answer.

"I did it because I wanted the "A" for me. Not for you, not for your dad, not for my professor. I did it for me! And that's what you have to do. You have to earn good grades because something deep inside of you wants it for yourself!" My voice was rising. "If I thought you couldn't do it, or that you were doing the best you could, I wouldn't be saying anything about it. But I know you're capable of doing much better than you've been doing." His grades had all gone down after the second six weeks. I realized that we were in the last stretch of the school year, but I didn't think it was too late. I didn't want him to think that we had given up on the possibility of him doing better. "Do you think you've done your best this year?"

"No," Tjai said. "I could have done better." He knew that I was referring that last "F" he had brought home on his report card.

I know you can do better," I said, in agreement. "But I also know that you have to want to do better... for yourself! Not for me, not for you dad, but for Tjai! Does that make sense?"

"Yes ma'am," he said quietly.

"You have an advantage that I didn't have, Tjai," I said.

"What do you mean?" he asked, looking up at me.

I noticed that his glasses were dirty, and again, I wondered how on earth he could see anything out of them. "I mean that you have parents who encourage you to do your best. Your dad and I stay on you because we want you to do your best. I didn't have that," I said. "My mom never gave me any encouragement. In fact she never thought that I would amount to very much."

"Why?" he asked, looking bewildered.

"Well," I began, "we didn't get along very well."

"What do you mean 'you didn't get along very well'?"

"She hated me... for a while," I said, knowing he didn't understand. I knew I wouldn't be able to explain to him either... not any time soon.

"What?" Tjai asked. He was obviously surprised to hear me say that. "Why do you say she hated you?"

"Well, she was angry with me about something... something I can't really tell you about right now."

"Why not?"

"Because you're too young to understand right now." I knew that if I told my twelve year old son that his grandmother hated me because her husband had sexually molested me, he wouldn't understand. I knew that if I told him how much she hated my father because he had killed her sister and her mother, he might be able to understand that. I knew, however, that he would never be able to comprehend why every time she looked at me, she saw that man... in me. "Aunt Meg thought I looked like my father," I tried to explain, "but, I really don't. Now, Debra, she does look like him." I took another sip of coffee.

Tjai waited.

"Everyone in our family hated him because of what he did," I said. "Even me."

He looked down at the newspaper, loosely scattered on the table.

"Aunt Meg, she really hated him. She hated him almost as much as I did. She saw him in me. I don't know why, but she did." I paused. "In a way, she hated me, too. So, she used to tell me that I was just like him…that I would never be anything. She would tell me that and more to my face. But you know what?"

"What?"

"Deep inside, I was determined that I was going to make a liar out of her! I was determined to be somebody! For me! I had to prove it to myself! So I worked hard to make "A's" because I wanted them for me. You understand that?"

He nodded, a different expression crossing his face.

"That's why I say you have an advantage that I didn't have," I said. "We tell you that you can be whatever you want to be. But you have to want more for yourself than anyone else, including me and your dad, could ever possibly want for you."

"Yes ma'am."

"You have to start now, you know? You can't wait until you get to high school to start studying and preparing yourself. You have to start now." I studied his face for a moment. He looked as if he was considering what I had said. "Go take out the trash," I said, finishing off my cup.

He got up from the table

"And go and clean those filthy glasses so you can see what you're doing!"

"Okay," He said, smiling.

Seven

I was in junior high school when gathered up enough nerve to tell my mom that my dad had been coming into the tiny room I slept in with my three brothers and "touching" me, during the night. Even before her disapproving eyes swept over me, I felt really filthy! It was as if my entire body had been soiled and I knew that I was unworthy of the love I so desperately wanted from Aunt Meg. I had failed her and I had failed myself. She hated me and I already knew that, but there seemed to be nothing I could do about it. After I summoned her from her slumber to break the devastating news to her, she had screamed obscenities, first at me and then at Harry. The next day, she acted as if she had forgotten all about it. I waited for her to say something more to him about the horrible thing he had done to me, but she didn't. I waited for her to tell him to get out, to divorce him for being unfaithful to her and tormenting me, but she didn't do anything... not to him, anyway. My life, however, became a living hell!

It seemed that an eternity passed. In that eternity, when the house became quiet and still, in the middle of the night, I would awaken to his deep, steady breathing, and the intermittent clicking of his teeth, like a nervous twitch, in my ears. As careful as he tried not to wake me, standing next to the bunk bed where I slept, I felt him each and every time he lifted my pajama top to touch rough finger tips on my developing breasts. I cringed, despising him and his touch! I knew that this was not "love" and if it was, I wanted no part of it! I didn't need to be loved like that. I would close my eyes tighter and lay as still as I could, afraid to breathe, lest he think I was a willing participant.

After a while, either Harry became braver or the impetuous touching was no longer enough to satisfy him. He began to tip into the bed with me, being careful, or so he thought, not to

136

wake me. Nausea swept over me as he took his act to an even lower level. When he crept out of my bunk bed, he left behind the residue of his having been there. I would lie there for a few minutes, tears filling my eyes, until I heard him climb back into bed in the adjoining room which he shared with my mom. When I heard the mattress squeak, I crawled out of bed and went to the bathroom to clean myself up. As I scrubbed myself and put on clean underwear, I asked God why such a horrible thing was happening to me. Somehow, I knew that He had to have heard me and I prayed that He would answer. I was a child, suddenly thrust into the life of an adult. I was still struggling to get accustomed to the pain created by Mama's absence. I was not ready for this new hurt and humiliation. It was overwhelming...

I don't know how long it went on like that, but one night, I decided that I could stand it no longer. I waited until after he had gone back to his bed and then I got up and followed him. I watched him climb into bed, on the side closest to the wall, his back turned to Aunt Meg. She was snoring lightly. I went over to the bed and touched her on the shoulder, waking her up.

"What's that matter?" she asked, groggily. She had been asleep for a couple of hours, at least.

Without a word, I pulled my wet panties down around my ankles, stepped out of them, and held them out to her. "He won't stop bothering me," I said, nodding at my dad. He didn't stir, but I knew he wasn't asleep. He couldn't have been. He had just laid down.

Aunt Meg knew what had happened. She sat up and took the underpants out of my hand. She sighed very deeply. "Harrison?"

"Huh?" he said, turning over slowly, as if he had actually been asleep. Sleepy-eyed, he sat up in the bed.

"Get up," Aunt Meg said. She got to her feet, cursing under her breath.

I stood frozen in front of her. This was it! He was finally going to have to tell the truth! He had been caught dead in the act! Now, explain your way out of this mess this time! I thought.

"Denise, go to bed!" my mom barked at me.

I was stunned! Go to bed? I didn't want to go to bed! I wanted to hear what my dad had to say in his defense! I wanted to see him weasel his way out of this like he had done so easily in the past. I wanted to hear him blame those soggy panties on my "tragic experiences of the past" and my being "emotionally unstable!" Go to bed? Disappointment overcame me. I frowned.

"Now!" she said, firmly.

I turned around and walked back to the bedroom with heavy footsteps.

The two of them went into the livingroom, out of earshot. They spoke in hushed tones. I guess they didn't want to wake up the whole house. I went to the bathroom to clean myself off. Then I went back into the bedroom, took a clean pair of panties from a drawer and put them on. As I climbed up into the top bunk, I strained my ears to hear the conversation that was going on in the livingroom. The voices were steadily rising.

"Or else, get out!" I heard Aunt Meg say, her shrill voice bouncing off the ceiling of the frame house.

My dad mumbled something.

She responded. It sounded as if she was talking under water.

He said something else.

Then there was silence.

I waited. A couple of minutes passed before I heard them come back into their bedroom. I peered through our open doorway. I saw their bedroom light go out. They had gone back to bed! Just like that? That was it? The weight of my burden threw me back onto my pillow. I had been defeated once again! I turned my face and cried into the crisp white pillowcase.

When I got up the next morning, I searched my mom's face for some indication of her thoughts or feelings. I didn't say anything to her, but I watched her closely. She avoided my gaze as much as possible. On the way to the junior high school both Wayne and I attended, the only sound in the car was that of the radio. Wayne, sitting in the back seat, sung along with the music, in his off-beat, off-pitch sort of way. I sat on the front seat, across from Aunt Meg. I could feel anger penetrating the air between us. I didn't know if that anger was hers, mine, or both! I was really teed off myself! I was the one who had been violated! I had every right to be angry! I knew that she was angry with me, as if it had been my fault. It wasn't my fault! I was convinced of that! Harry was the one who had wronged both me and Aunt Meg! Like me, she should have been angry with him! My face grew crimson as I considered bringing this to her attention. Of course, I never said a word. I knew that Wayne nor my other brothers had any idea about the awful sin I had been a part of. I hoped they would never find out. It was too humiliating for me to share with anyone! I felt very relieved when my mom dropped us off in front of the big red-brick school building.

All day long, I thought about the previous night, unable to understand why nothing more had come of Harry's being caught red-handed! What was it going to take for my mom to look through the lies and deceit and see the filth? Why couldn't she see it? He was a sick, perverted man! But she couldn't, or perhaps, wouldn't see it! So he got away, scott-free, a little while longer.

I have often wondered what he thought about when he looked at me. I wondered time and time again if he ever felt any remorse for what he did to me. In a way, I don't think he ever fully realized the impact of what he did. At times, I have found myself looking upon him as a victim, somehow. That may be hard for some people to understand. I have considered that perhaps he is a victim of some sickness, some perversion, which was beyond his control. I have even wondered if he overcame his perversion, while secretly thanking the Lord that He blessed me with sons, instead of daughters, which would have required my constant vigil, under the circumstances.

As that particular demon found his way out of it familiar hiding place, I found myself slipping into a dark hole out of which I was not quite sure I could write myself. The mushroom grew enormous inside of me. Almost larger than life, it took up space where my internal organs were supposed to be! My kidneys were pushed out of place. I felt the pressure. I became out of sync! I prayed for God to touch me, to squelch the mushroom and move my organs back into place!

Sometime in July of 1997, Darrell went out of town for a few days. The timing was very bad. He was absent during a time when I really needed him! Although I knew that he wasn't interested in my thoughts or my written rantings, I needed him to hold me... or rather, to hold onto me. I was having difficulty holding onto myself! Just when I was about to crumble under the pressure, God stepped in. I knew that it was He. Darrell called and told me that I had just "popped" into his mind! As tears fell from my eyes, I told him that I was really glad about that. I knew that he didn't want me to be upset and he really believed that my writing was probably doing more harm than good. He felt that to put my nightmare on paper was to dredge up old memories and bring myself a great deal of pain. I tried to make him understand that although what he said was partially true, I still needed to write, to get it all out! He told me that if my faith in God was as strong as I professed it to be, I should be able to give my past, no matter how terrible it is, to God, and just forget about it. I thought that was pretty incredible. Darrell had no idea just how hard I had tried to do just that! But I couldn't. I couldn't just give to the Lord. I was compelled to write about it. I believe that God put it in my heart to write about it. In some way, I believed that the words were meant to be in print. The experiences and their overcoming were meant to be shared with those who have yet learned to overcome their own experiences. God had carefully preserved me so that I could share my testimony.

Even though it seemed to tear me apart at the seams, writing helped me to "unpack" my emotions. I learned that ignoring the past will not make it go away! Darrell doesn't know that, but he is not alone. Several times, he has encouraged me to stop dwelling on the past because he believed that it would somehow miraculously disappear! Bad things, he told me, happen to people every day. As a firefighter, my husband witnesses tragedy nearly every shift. He sees people cut, stabbed, shot, burned, devastated and lifeless! I wouldn't dare minimize his own experiences, but they are very, very different from mine. No one physically abused him! No one sexually molested him! No one brutally snuffed out his darling mother's life, before his very eyes! Thank God, that she is alive and well! Darrell may not have realized it, but our life experiences have been dramatically different!

I used to feel sorry for myself. I felt badly that I didn't have my mother to talk to, laugh with, or cry with. I couldn't see her smile or call her up on the phone to tell her of my joys and sorrows. No one got to walk her up the aisle as the"mother of the bride." She wasn't there when my sons were born. She didn't see them take their first tiny steps or hear their first utterances of "mama" and the infamous "no!" I have often regretted that she never got to share in the childhood that I had or to witness the woman that I became. There is some consolation in that she was possibly somewhere watching me as I grew and developed. Maybe she did see the mistakes I made before I made them and wished that she could have influenced my choices. Perhaps she was at my high school graduation when I stood before my classmates and delivered the salutatorial address that I knew, even as a little girl, I would grow up to deliver. She could have recognized in my life, the life that she would have possibly chosen for herself -- without the nastiness, of course! What parent has not tried to emit some of their own hopes and dreams into the lives of their children?

I don't know when I stopped feeling sorry for myself, but at some time or another, I did. It became apparently clear to me that the person I became, as an adult, was the result of the many experiences, both positive and negative, I had had in my life. Even though I had tragically lost my parents, God had given me something else. That something else didn't necessarily take Mama's place, but it allowed me to express myself. That something else was the gift of music He gave to me. God's grace turned the negative effects of the tragedy into a positive medium of beautiful expression in the words and music I have written and sung throughout the years. When, at the age of eight years, I considered my loss and asked "What now?" God answered,

"Now, you can journey on. Now, you can sing a new song." When I agonized over being criticized and persecuted for telling the horrid truth about being molested, God was saying to me, "Although you must grow up quickly, you will grow up stronger than you thought you'd be." After having married into yet another nightmare and seemingly increased my own suffering, God opened the door and let me walk over the threshold to freedom. As I walked, He encouraged, "You can keep going, now that you know you must trust me for everything you want and need in your life!" Even as I recalled the anguish I felt after being attacked in my classroom, I heard God speaking to me, His voice sounding like a tranquil melody, "Even amidst your greatest trial, I have continued to walk with you and to guide you...Now, you can be my witness!"

Years later, after Mama died, I would find myself wondering why God had spared my life. Throughout the years, I have done just that. I wondered why the fatal bullet found its way into Grandmama's chest instead of mine. I no longer have to question His motives. I have gotten my answer. He was keeping me in order that I might someday fulfill a higher purpose. Now I know that the door which Debra helped to open had no other choice than to swing wide! The glue that held it shut for many, many years was not permanent. It was God's intention that time would wear it away, like those rushing waters of the Pacific, smoothing boulders into pebbles in time. The waters of my life have been tumultuous, but not overwhelming! I have been down, but never out! At my weakest moment, God sent His angels to lift me up.

One day, while living in Los Angeles, I had come home to the small single-apartment building where Tjai and I had been living for the past couple of months. As my toddler and I walked away from the car I had just parked in front of the house which sat to the right-front of our apartment, I had the feeling that we were being watched. I turned around to see a man, in a dark, trench coat and hat, standing on the sidewalk, looking in our direction. I hadn't been in LA long and I was still a little nervous about being out there on my own. Almost immediately, my heart began to pound in my chest as I thought, "What now?" I looked down at my son, who obviously had not even noticed the stranger. As my hand tightened around his, I swore under my breath that if the man tried anything, I would literally whip his butt to protect my son. When I looked back to see what he was doing, he was gone! Just like that!

A few days later, I relayed the story to Ella Givens, a retired teacher, who was also the organist who accompanied me at the United Methodist Church where I was playing. Ella, ever the Christian Scientist, promptly assured me that the man was an "angel," sent to watch over Tjai and me. I was silently disturbed at her analysis and did not comment. I didn't, for one minute, believe that the gravely-dressed character was any angel...at least, not then. Now, I can't help but wonder if he, indeed, was an angel. When I think back to that day, the man was just standing there, a look of calm respite on his face. He didn't make a move toward or away from Tjai and me. He just seemed to be "checking," perhaps to see if we were "okay." Dear Ella, she always spoke with such eccentricity, at times, I hardly ever knew how to take her. But, I loved her just the same. She had an insight that not very many people have. I'm not saying that just because she thought that I was special, but she did! Often she even called me an angel!

It is my sincerest belief that God had a purpose for my life, even before I was born. He knew that my life would be overcast by the trials and tribulations as it has been. He also knew that I would be tossed and torn just as I have been. In His omniscience, He knew that the mechanism I unknowingly used to "lock away" the past would kick in at just the right moment, precisely as it did. But God knew something more about me. He knew what He had given to me while I was still in my mother's womb. He had given me a spiritual strength that the deafening blast of gunshots could not shatter! That strength was impenetrable even by physical or sexual abuse! It could not be broken! The "seed" of the Spirit was planted deep within my soul, deeper than any amount of suffering could ever reach! After the suffering and the dense fog had lifted, a beautiful blossom of faith grew!

In your own life, if you stopped and seriously considered where you have been, you would realize that only by God's grace and mercy, you have been able to come to this moment in time. Oh, Satan has always been watching for the right moment to jump in and tear you and I asunder, but God has never been far away, waiting to see what choices we would make and how we would fare under pressure. One thing I have learned throughout this miraculous life of mine is to trust Him. I have learned to put more of my faith in someone who not only knows me, but who also knows that the future holds for me. That is what God wants us to do. No matter what happens around us or to us, He wants us to yet trust Him. That is the measure of our faith...trust in God. Job, a witness for the Lord, put it in a nutshell when he said, "Though they slay me, yet will I trust Him." In my opinion, he was in a far worse condition than I have ever been. If he could continue to trust God, in the midst of his miserable state, who am I, or you, for that matter, **not** to trust God?

There are pictures, still vivid, in your mind, of some trial or tribulation that you, too, have faced. There is someone whom you trusted and because of their infidelity or deception, you have found it difficult to forgive them... perhaps even impossible! I have had to draw upon strength I didn't even know I possessed in order to forgive those whom I held responsible for my own anguish. It has not been an easy task, but then, forgiving is not an easy act to perform. That is probably because even when we say we "forgive," we never really "forget!" I don't really think God expects us to forget. Pastor Thompson once said that to forget means that we really haven't forgiven. After all, we would have to remember what it is that was done wrong in order to truly forgive the person who is guilty of the wrongdoing. When he put it like that, it made perfect sense to me. The memories will always be a part of me because they helped to mold me into the woman that I am today. However, along the way, I realized that those who have wronged me, I must forgive! That is the only way God can bring us into the manifestation of who He intended for us to be!

Where does forgiveness begin? When I made a conscientious decision to forgive my father for taking my mother away from me, I asked my aunt, Patricia, to locate a picture of him for me. I had not even seen a picture of him in thirty-one years. I knew that the sight of him would summon emotions I had not ever wanted to experience again. I called "Aunt Tisa" and asked her to bring a picture of Tony to choir rehearsal with her one Thursday night. When I arrived at the church, she met me with three photographs of him. When my aunt handed them to me, I didn't look at them right away. I went ahead with rehearsal, all the while, voices in my head warning me that I really ought not to look at them. Something, around the base of the mushroom, argued, "You need to look at them! You need to see him! You must face him! Finally!"

After rehearsal, I took the pictures out of my purse and sat down on a pew in the church. I took a deep breath and turned them over in my hands. The eyes that stared back at me were like Debra's. "Humph," I murmured to myself. "There you are."

Aunt Tisa was watching me, quietly, as if she perhaps wanted to give me time to absorb the pictures.

I sighed deeply, looking from one snapshot to the other, remembering the man who was pictured sitting in an early-model Bel-Air and again standing next to my mother, on a nightclub stage where their group "Flip Clayton, the Houseshakers and the Flipperettes!" had performed. On one picture, I saw Tony, but the face, the hair, the eyes, the smile were my brother Michael's, dark and exotic-looking. On another, my youngest brother, Ronnie's pug nose jumped off the picture at me. Debra has that same nose, I thought. I studied his hand and the cigarette which seemed to dance in it. That same hand had pulled the trigger on a .38 and changed my whole life. He was smiling, but the smile was not a victorious one. I saw something in the dark eyes that looked like discomfort… like pain. The eyes betrayed the smile. Tony's eyes were windows to a sadly dark soul. It suddenly occurred to me that he had not been victorious after all. He had been merely an instrument. Satan had used him to do his dirty work! He had used him to take Mama away in an attempt to destroy us - Wayne, Michael, Ronnie and me! Satan had only partially succeeded. True, Mama was physically gone, but her Spirit, the Spirit of God and of love that she had passed on to us was yet alive! That spirit had kindled the tiny seed of faith she planted the numerous times she had taken me and my brothers to Sunday School and to church, and the many, many times she had sung "What is This?" in her own church choir.

"What is this," Mama had sung, "that I can feel deep down inside? What is this, that keeps setting my soul on fire? Whatever it is, it won't let me, it won't let me hold my peace!"

Many times, I had heard Mama sing, "It makes me love my enemies, and I know it makes me love my friends. And it won't let me be ashamed, to tell the world I've been born again!"

As I came face-to-face with Tony, I understood what Mama meant. She had not held her peace. She was still speaking to, in, and through me! I had lost Mama's physical presence, but Tony had suffered a loss more great and unimaginable than mine. He had lost his very soul! I began to feel sorry for him.

"Are you alright?" Aunt Tisa asked, with a gentle smile on her lips.

I nodded my head. Somehow I knew I was on my way to being just fine!

"The Lord is my strength and my shield; my heart trusted in Him, and I am helped; therefore my heart greatly rejoiceth; and with my song will I praise Him. Psalm 28:7

I forgave Tony that night. I forgave him, even though I didn't forgive his monstrous deed. In all of his mean selfishness, he still belonged to God. He had not done what God wanted him to do, but he was His, just the same. He was just one of many who have resisted God's calling to a life of salvation. The choice he had made was his and he had made it freely. My choice was to forgive him because I needed that forgiveness in my own life. Almost immediately, I felt the mushroom begin to shrink. Aloud, I said the words, "I forgive you," and my breathing became easier. I began to summon others to mind who had caused me pain and anguish at some time in my life. "Travis, I forgive you. There is no need to tell you what you have or have not done. You already know. But, in spite of it all, I forgive you." I could feel more space becoming available inside. "Harry, I forgive you, because if I don't, I can in no way fulfill the promise I made, not only to Aunt Meg, but to God, that I would take care of you. So, I forgive you, too." That was probably more difficult for me to do than to forgive Tony because he is still very much a part of my present. Perhaps some may wonder how I could, in fact, forgive my dad for his sin against me, but I believe that God would have had it no other way! We must open our hearts completely to the will of God in order to receive the blessings which He has for our lives. He has told us that in order for us to be truly forgiven for our own sins, we must forgive those who despitefully use us. Without forgiveness, our lives can never be "complete" and we can never be "whole." I went on and on, verbalizing my forgiveness of any and everyone I could think of who had ever hurt me. I knew that it was what I had to do. For the very first time in my life, I was able to do it!

Now that the door has been completely opened, there is no need to reseal it. There is no need to lock away any residuals of the past. I realize there are probably many who will learn things about me that they never imagined to be true. Members of my very own family will no doubt be shocked by some of what I've written within these covers. I hope that they will understand and take to heart the healing that I have experienced as a result of opening the door to my past. Perhaps they, too, will achieve a measure of healing in their own lives. At least, I pray that they will.

"We are troubled on every side, yet not distressed; we are perplexed, but not in despair; Persecuted, but not forsaken; cast down, but not destroyed." II Cor. 8-9

Eight

One evening in September, 1996, Ophelia was at my house, visiting. As we sat across from each other at the dining table, she noticed a lump on the left side of my throat. "How long have you had that?" she asked, cocking her head to one side.

Subconsciously, I put my hand up to feel the fleshy bulge I had noticed a week or two earlier. "I don't know."

She got up and came around the table to feel it. "That feels like a goiter," she observed. "You need to have that checked.

"You think so?" I asked, laughing uncomfortably. I didn't admit to my friend that I had been worried about it, but I had. In fact, I had been preoccupied with it ever since I had noticed that, at times, my throat had become very sore, almost so sore that I had trouble swallowing. Singing had become a challenge with the lump moving into the path my vocal chords had been accustomed to using.

At Ophelia's suggestion, I made an appointment a couple of days later and went to see my family doctor about the knot in my throat. The kindly, soft-spoken man didn't even feel it when he pressed his warm hands to my neck. He prescribed something for inflammation, probably more for my emotional health than for the actual problem. After I had been taking the medication for a month or so, I called the doctor again. The lump had gotten larger!

Upon my next visit to his office, the doctor referred me to a specialist. As it turned out, I was able to go in to see him that same day. Anxiously, I drove to his office, which was not very far away from my family doctor's office. When the specialist examined me, almost immediately, he exclaimed, "You've got a growth of some kind there!"

"A growth?" I asked.

"Yes," he said, sitting down on a stool opposite from me on the exam table. "It could be a goiter or some type of tumor."

Tumor? Tumor? What kind of tumor? I asked myself, totally ignoring the "goiter" diagnosis.

He sensed my apprehension. "It could be either one. If it's a goiter, we can probably treat it with medication. If not, surgery may be necessary."

"Oh," I said, looking out of the window at the changing leaves on a nearby poplar tree.

He went on. "Of course, we'll try the medication first to see if that will take care of the problem." He began scribbling on a pad in his lap. "I want you to begin this medication immediately," he said. "I will see you back in about three weeks and we'll check to see how you're doing." He stood up, tore the prescription from his pad and handed it to me.

When I left the office, I was shaken. I drove the thirty-eight miles to school, but I was obviously in no mood to teach that day. I went through the day feeling very much out of sync.

At home, Darrell was very supportive. He kept telling me to trust God that everything would be alright. That became increasingly difficult to do as it became harder and harder to sing, whether I was at church or in rehearsal with the gospel music group I had been singing with for the past year. I felt myself becoming more and more downhearted about my condition. I began to pray for God's deliverance. At the time, I did not remind Him of the obstacles He had brought me around in the past. That was probably because it had not yet occurred to me that He had actually been responsible. I simply asked Him to heal my body, my mind and my broken spirit.

"...He heareth the cry of the afflicted." Job 34:28b

Each time I opened my mouth to sing praises to the Lord, Satan tightened his grip on the lump in throat. At Monday night rehearsals with the group, my tears of anguish would often be uncontrollable. My range had changed and I could no longer sing the loftier notes I had sung since I could well remember. I moved from the soprano section to sing with the tenors. On Thursday nights, when I rehearsed with my church choir, I continued to teach songs of Zion to my choir members, even though the pain in my throat was almost unbearable! On Sunday mornings, I sang as hard as I could, ending up hoarse at the end of worship service. I decided that whatever was left of my voice would be used for God's glory! Although I was still very frustrated that my instrument of praise had been afflicted, I decided that I would go on and sing anyhow! I refused to let Satan stop me from praising the Lord! In the meantime, I prayed daily that God would restore His gift to me.

The specialist referred me to a surgeon. The surgeon, Dr. Whitman, was a warm-hearted man who sat and talked at length with Darrell and I about my upcoming surgery. I expressed to him my concern about the surgery, which would involve literally "cutting my throat," and possibly ending my singing career.

With obvious concern, he told me that although he would be doing just that, he would take every precaution so as not to sever the nerves which led to my vocal chords. He did say, however, that the operation was a sensitive one and he could not guarantee that my voice would not be affected. "But," he said, "I am praying that God will guide my hands during the operation so that you will be able to sing again one day!"

I smiled and my spirit leapt within!

The surgery was performed on November 7, 1996. Before the anesthesia took me to a land of dreams, Dr. Whitman squeezed my hand and told me that everything would be fine. I was counting on him and God to make good on that promise!

Afterwards, the doctor told me that the tumor which had attached itself to my left thyroid, had been the size of a man's fist. In my throat! "No wonder," he exclaimed, "you had difficulty singing!" "Swallowing must have been hell, too!" he said, smiling.

I tried to return his smile. He had **no** idea! As I watched him leave my hospital room, I thanked God for being there, in the operating room with me, in Dr. Whitman's hands. Now all I had to do was wait to see if my voice would, indeed, return.

"Wait on the Lord: be of good courage, and he shall strengthen thine heart: wait, I say, on the Lord." Psalm 27:14

It has been almost a year since I prayed and asked God, as the anesthesia took effect, to cover my vocal chords with his Holy anointing. Ten months have passed since I woke up to the agonizing pain which seared through my throat and nearly singed my faith. With each passing day, I have felt God's healing, one cell at a time, nerve ending by nerve ending. Today, still not yet one hundred percent, I am thankful for the fulfillment of His promise... not that He would return my soprano voice to me, but that He would restore unto me the joy of my salvation! Restoration of my voice was not a promise. That was a blessing!

Last Sunday, Tracey, a member of my choir, asked me if I would sing "When We Get Over There," a song I had sung with the choir during rehearsal a couple of weeks earlier. She told me that she wanted to tape it because she had promised to send it to someone. I always try to make a point of doing what someone asks me to do because you never know why they're asking. If God had put it on her heart, who was I not to do it?

After the choir had processed into the sanctuary, I began to play the introduction. At the same time, I whispered a prayer to God for strength to sing His praise. I believe that He heard my prayer because I sung the song as I had never sung it before! Even before my surgery! Even before my tumor! The voice that spilled out of my soul was beautiful and new to me! "Oh what joy!" I sang. "Oh what peace! When we get over there! Oh what joy!" As I prepared myself to sing the highest note in the song, one I had **never** been able to sing before, I opened my mouth and heard it ring out all over the sanctuary, "Oh what peace!"

All over the church, the Spirit of God moved. Tears ran down my cheeks as He wrapped His arms of love around me. "Thank you Lord!" I said, audibly. "Thank you Jesus!" In my ears, rang echoes of praise throughout the choir and congregation.

151

A few days later, Deacon Brown, my good friend and fellow choir member, would chuckle and say to me, "Girl, you were somewhere else last Sunday!"

But I knew that he had said more than he realized. Not only had I been "somewhere" else, "someone" else had been with me! I had felt God's arms around me, arms which reached down into my soul, through the muck and mire, through the heartache and pain, through the sickness and sadness. At once, I knew what the songwriter meant when he penned the words, It is well, it is well with my soul!

"Thou wilt keep him in perfect peace, whose mind is stayed on thee: because he trusteth in thee." Isaiah 26:3

I once told my husband that one of the worse things in the world to me was to want to sing and not be able to. I have come one step closer to the truth. It is far worse not to be able to use the gift to praise the gift-giver! Satan has tried to put me in that predicament in more ways than one! He has tried to conquer my soul by placing obstacles in my path which would have sent an ordinary man into a tailspin! I am not saying that I am extraordinary. I'm just someone willing to share my testimony for the good and edification of someone else. I realize that Satan's pursuit neither began nor ended with me. We are all targets of his wanton affections. I am no different from you or anyone else. When I was born, he began seeking after my soul. Perhaps he suspected that God had great intentions for me. Maybe he had an inkling that the testimony I would be able to give would be strong enough to help others to realize God in their lives, some of whom might otherwise shrink from His calling. Satan knows a lot of things about us. But I would venture to say that God knows more! He knows what you're going through and He knows how you can get through it. He has already told us how to overcome.

I have come to the realization that I am an overcomer. I have been through the storm and the rain, as the song says, but I made it! I believe that God intended for me to do so in order that I could be a witness to others who are yet going through their own storm. What better testimony than that of having overcome? The reasons are crystal clear to me now. The striking result of the bitter and painful past is the glorious testimony it has yielded!

"For whatsoever is born of God overcometh the world: and this is the victory that overcometh the world, even our faith." I John 5:4

The child I used to be was frail and alone, bewildered by the seeming unfairness of life. Without my mother, I felt disadvantaged, almost handicapped. I knew that life would never be the same and I was right. It never was. After seeking solace in a new home, I met with further disappointment which could have left me hopeless. God saw to it that a seed of hope was planted deep within my soul. Throughout the years, the faith that grew enabled me to walk on through the storm and the rain. Meanwhile, God kept sending His angels to lift up my bowed down head and enlighten my heart. That is what He does. He sends us people to remind us that no matter how bad our circumstances become, we can still overcome them!

My mother would be proud of the person I have become. I am sure of that. She would be glad that I had endured the test of the life which was placed before me. Despite the odds, I have been able to keep afloat. The Word of God has, in my darkest hour, sustained me. I am thankful for God's presence in my life, even during times I felt deserted. I know now that He never, ever left me! He was never far from me, as He promised. I feel like shouting for though weeping endured for many a night, it is now morning and joy has finally come! I no longer regret the journey because I know that I had to go there in order to get here. I can say, in the words of the old Negro Spiritual, "I wouldn't take nothin' for my journey right now!"

After a long hard night on duty at the fire station, Darrell came home around eight o'clock in the morning. He found me sitting in front of my computer, busily trying to finish up my manuscript. He came into the room, sat down in a chair beside me and told me that he had something he wanted to tell me. I looked up and smiled. I was feeling pretty high, having finally gotten to what I felt was the end of my thoughts. With a thoughtful expression on his face, he told me that on the way home, he had thought about something he felt I might be able to use in my book.

I stopped typing and looked at him.

What my husband told me was one of the most profound ideas that I had heard in quite some time. He said, "God puts people, good or bad, in our lives by design: For a reason, for a season and for the rest of our lives."

The words struck a chord deep within me. Immediately, I turned back to the computer keyboard and added them to my manuscript.

What Darrell had said was so full of truth! I thought about everyone I had ever known. No matter who they were or how they had affected my life, they had all touched it and in the process, had become part of the "me" that now exists. It was true. God had put each person in my life, for good or bad, better or worse, richer or poorer, in sickness or in health, for as long as I live. Each person had contributed something to the dimensions that became my character. Each person came, touched my life, and left their distinguishing shadow upon my memory. Even after separation by life, death, or distance, they were and will always be a part of who I am. It matters not the reason, or the season, but it is, beyond a shadow of a doubt ... for the rest of my life.

"And we know that all things work together for good to them that love God, to them who are the called according to his purpose." Romans 8:28

"The past has been taken care of by yesterday," I once heard a revival preacher say. I wanted to tell him that I agreed with him. Yesterday has indeed taken care of the past. We need only to reconcile ourselves with our yesterdays and acknowledge them as part of who and what we are today. There is no need to fear the past. It only comes back to haunt us if we fail to deal with it in real terms. And then it only haunts us because we cannot fully accept the implications the past has on our present and future. What effect does past experience have on us? I would have to say a dramatic one! Those experiences all serve to shape and mold us into who we are. Even if the experiences are negative and painful, they still contribute to the facets of our lives. It is when we allow God to lead and guide us that the outcome is good, regardless of the ingredients that went in ahead of time.

I have concluded that God's purpose is the only one for my life, the life that He has touched, anointed and preserved. It must be used for His purpose alone. I am grateful for the opportunity to share this testimony with others in hopes that they, too, will be able to open the door to their own pasts and allow God to help them unpack and discard those things which have long ago outlived their usefulness. Only then can we truly be used by Him.

"The Lord is my strength and my shield; my heart trusted in Him, and I am helped: therefore my heart greatly rejoiceth; and with my song will I praise him."
Psalm 28:7

In memory of my beloved pastor, mentor and friend, the late Reverend Tony Thompson, Jr., who was called Home to Glory on December 28, 1997. The candle has been extinguished and the flame no longer burns, but the light will never die.